Dear Work

Dear

Work

SOMETHING
HAS TO
CHANGE!

SARA ROSS

PAGE TWO

Cataloguing in publication information is available from Library and Archives Canada.
ISBN 978-1-77458-319-7 (hardcover)
ISBN 978-1-77458-246-6 (ebook)
ISBN 978-1-77458-336-4 (audiobook)
Also available in paperback

Page Two
pagetwo.com

Edited by Kendra Ward
Copyedited by Shyla Seller
Proofread by Alison Strobel
Jacket design by Peter Cocking
Interior design by Cameron McKague
Printed and bound in Canada by Friesens
Distributed in Canada by Raincoast Books
Distributed in the US and internationally by Macmillan

HARDCOVER EDITION
23 24 25 26 27 5 4 3 2 1

dearworkbook.com

For you, Mom

Contents

DEAR WORK

I need to start by saying, you are an important part of my life and have provided me with a deep sense of purpose and joy. You have allowed me to test myself and express myself and have given me a way to contribute to something bigger. You have challenged me to learn and grow—to do work that matters to me, and I am truly grateful.

But admittedly, Work, it's getting harder to stay connected to the good things. Too often you take over my life. And when this happens, my priorities, happiness, and even my confidence seem to hinge on you. It's impossible to ignore that the pace, the intensity, and the sacrifices all come at a high price. I know it, and those who love me have let me know it, too.

The thing is, the satisfaction and energy I get when you are going well are not far-off memories. Some days are amazing and I remember exactly what I love about you. But if I'm honest, the gaps between the good days are getting bigger and most days it feels like I'm just treading water.

What scares me most is that the harder I work, the further behind I feel. There rarely seems to be enough time for everything. I feel stuck in this never-ending cycle where the demands keep coming but the bar of success keeps rising, and I am tired.

Is this what I want my life to be? Do I have what it takes, or do I need to temper my drive—to stop giving so much or being so passionate? There must be another option. I love you, Work, or I used to, but something has to change.

Exhaustedly, but still yours,

Introduction

THE LETTER you just read lives in a wooden box tucked away in the corner of my office closet. That box is full of letters I've written throughout my life. Now, you may be thinking, "Isn't the purpose of writing a letter to send it?" Usually, yes. When I have things on my mind that I can't sort out or emotions that weigh heavily on my heart, I write letters—and I don't send them. The process creates space between me and my experiences and helps me see things with a fuller perspective. I have written them since I was young, and I do it to this day.

The only difference with the letter you just read was that I had always written to people up to that point. But the day I wrote to "Work," I was feeling both maxed out by the pressure of multiple impending deadlines and worn out by the hours I had been putting in to meet them. I was just about to text friends to cancel plans (for the second time) we had for later that evening when, distractedly reaching for my phone, I knocked over my coffee, spilling it onto the floor. As I tried to clean up before it stained the carpet, I was overcome with a sense of utter frustration and total exhaustion—and in hindsight, fear. Not because of some spilled coffee, but because in that moment, I had to admit to myself that after I had experienced near burnout in my last sales role, changed jobs, and careers for that matter, I again found myself on the same path.

More maddening was that I'd had multiple experiences before this instance prompting me to make changes. My body was throwing up all sorts of red flags warning me that I was pushing it too hard and not caring for it enough. And still, I couldn't seem to break out of the cycle of overworking and continuously sacrificing the things that mattered. Deep down, I was scared that the only way I could be successful was to keep going like this. And if I couldn't, what would that mean for my future goals? But if I did, what would be the cost?

Our Relationship to Work

Like any relationship, our relationship to work can be complicated. This is especially true if you are someone who loves your work, feels it is a meaningful and important element of your life, and are committed to being successful at it. The challenge is we give and give, expecting work to reciprocate our commitment. We wait for it to make us feel worthy, to recognize our efforts, and to signal that we've done enough for the day and that it is okay to take a break. And when work just keeps coming, regardless of our capacity or circumstances, we blame it for consuming and depleting us, for causing us to doubt ourselves, and for not allowing us to be happy.

While many important factors contribute to your relationship with work, let's be very clear: no matter how much you give to your work and sacrifice in the name of passion, dedication, and loyalty, *work cannot love you back*. There is only one *person* in your relationship with work, which means that the only one who can fulfill your plea for change is you. If you wait for work to change, you'll always feel stuck, which is exactly where I found myself. As I sat on my office floor that day, I realized that when it came to work and my relationship with it, something needed to change. And I knew it wasn't just me that felt this way.

The Survival Zone
. . . .

At the time of writing my letter to work, I was the global head of leadership research and innovation at an organization where I regularly assessed, trained, and coached leaders and their people in the skills of emotional intelligence. While many were successful and enjoyed their work, again and again, in hushed voices, as if they were admitting to something that only they experienced, clients would make a confession. Regardless of how passionate they were about their career or how committed they were to their job, they often felt stuck in what I refer to as the "survival zone." While it wasn't all of the time, it was too often and that was the problem.

Some explained being in survival mode as having too much to do and not enough of anything for the rest of their lives. For others, it was being stuck on "autopilot"—existing but not fully living—leaving them disillusioned with work and little hope for change in the future. Much like myself, many experienced it as the pattern of pushing themselves to the brink of exhaustion, dialing it back, promising themselves and others they'd create better balance in the future, only to find the frustrating cycle repeating too soon. And then there were those who had run on fumes for so long that they'd hit empty, and as a result had moved into a different zone altogether—burnout.

I distinctly recall a conversation with a client who depicted the cycle of the survival zone the following way: "I used to love my work but now, night after night, I fall into bed drained, only to wake up exhausted. Looking at the week ahead, my mindset has become to simply get through it. I find myself wishing the days away, waiting for the weekend. Then I miss out on most of the weekend, either because I'm thinking about the work I should be doing—or dreading the work that awaits me in the week ahead."

Given the estimate that most people will spend close to 90,000 hours working, that is a lot of time to be wished away, wanting things to change, and waiting for a weekend, vacation, or retirement.

There was a longing in the stories I heard. Following a keynote I delivered for a business association, a gentleman approached me and with notable shame in his voice asked, "I want to be a better leader for my people but most days I just feel too tired to do it. Is there something wrong with me?" We aren't broken, but with stress, burnout, and job resignation being reported at record highs, something about how we are working certainly isn't working.

Shortly after writing my letter to work, I started BrainAmped, a leadership research firm to better understand what change needed to happen when it came to our relationship with work. I dove deeply into the academic research. I administered surveys, pored over company performance reviews and leadership assessments, and conducted dozens and dozens of interviews. All the way through, checking and calibrating my findings with companies I advised, audiences I spoke to, and clients I coached. After all the research and testing, including through a global pandemic, what I learned about our relationship to work is the following:

1 The experience of feeling stuck in the survival zone is pervasive.

2 While there is a desire to change the relationship between over-working and under-living, it is often hindered by the general belief that succeeding in one area requires sacrificing another. To excel at work means settling for an element of exhaustion (because this is the only way to get everything done) and having a fuller, more energy-fueled life requires settling for an element of mediocrity at work (because there is no way to get everything done). Either way, there is always an undesirable trade-off.

3 As prevalent as points one and two are, there are everyday people working in similarly stress-filled environments that do so with a sense of *aliveness* and thus are having a very different experience with work.

The Stand-Out Zone
. . . .

These "everyday people" described in point three range from bankers, lawyers, and air traffic controllers to surgeons, dentists, and engineers. Some are leaders at Fortune 500 companies, and others are individual contributors working for non-profits. They also include nurses, service operators, teachers, owners of small businesses, and ambitious entrepreneurs working to make their side hustle a full-time gig.

To be clear, it's not that these everyday people are charismatic, extroverted, peppy go-getters bounding out of bed every day because they love work so much (many are quite the opposite). Nor are they untouched by stress or avoid getting pulled into the survival zone entirely; they experience their fair share of both. Rather, the difference is they don't get stuck feeling trapped in trade-offs or defined by their circumstances. While there are always some sacrifices that need to be made, they recognize more readily when these sacrifices result in working from the survival zone and deliberately devise an exit strategy to get back out. As a result, they spend more time working from what I call the "stand-out zone."

While working in the survival zone is predicated on exhaustion, disillusionment, and sacrifice-based trade-offs, the stand-out zone is the opposite. It is characterized by deliberate choices and actions where people feel motivated and capable of bringing *their* best to what they do in the most energizing and healthy way. Whether with a quiet, caring groundedness or palpable state of enthusiasm, these everyday people working in the stand-out zone infuse a sense of aliveness into the projects they work on, the people they work with, and the pursuits that matter to them both at work *and* outside of it.

As you can imagine, if it was doable for some to work and feel this way, even while their colleagues were stuck in the survival zone, I wanted to know: was this something anyone could learn to do? What was the source of the aliveness they radiated? How did they maintain that spark, especially in high-stress environments? And perhaps most importantly, how did they seem to live a fulfilling life without losing their foothold on success?

Simply put, the answer to my first question is yes—anyone can learn how to work more reliably in the stand-out zone. But be forewarned, it's not as simple as working less and resting more.

To help you understand how to stop spinning your wheels, there are a couple of truths that I must acknowledge. First, you *can* run on fumes in the survival zone for a long time. Second, you can accomplish great things even when you're exhausted. In fact, what is clear from the data is that people working from the survival zone often meet the same performance outcomes as those working from the stand-out zone. Unfortunately, this leads people to believe that the only reason they are achieving their outcomes is because of the trade-offs they are making. However, exhaustion and excellence are not mutually exclusive. As such, *it is also true* that you don't have to be exhausted to accomplish great things. The biggest difference between the stand-out zone and the survival zone isn't *what* people achieve; it is *how* people meet those goals. In particular, what their *workdays look like* and what their *lives feel like* are very different. Consider the table below: which zone are you most often working from? Or perhaps the more important question: what would be possible if you worked more consistently from the stand-out zone?

When Working from the Survival Zone You Generally...	When Working from the Stand-Out Zone You Generally...
Don't feel you have enough time for the important things in your work and life.	Prioritize the important things in your work and life.
Feel a compulsive push to work.	Feel a positive pull toward work.
Have loose work-life boundaries, so you feel you should respond to work at all times.	Set clear work-life boundaries and respond to work at appropriate times.

Work excessively.	Work efficiently.
Say yes to every request, regardless of your priorities.	Say no to requests outside your priorities.
Feel guilty, anxious, or distracted in other parts of life when not working.	Feel present and engaged in other parts of life when not working.
Feel like you've never done enough.	Know you can't do it all.

Getting the Most from This Book
. . . .

Taking steps toward creating or maintaining a healthier and more fulfilling relationship to work becomes easier when you start by looking at human and organizational behavior through the lens of brain science. While I am neither a neuroscientist nor a psychologist, my goal is to distill only the most relevant and applicable studies and convey them in the most actionable way. As such, there are a few things to clarify about the focus of this book.

First, this isn't a book about "getting back to" what used to work. Following significant disruption and change—as in a pandemic—it is natural for you to try to rediscover your old normal. Unfortunately, this approach will just cause problems. Although you must look to the past for clues to your successes, simply trying to recreate what worked previously won't be enough to work in healthy, high-performing ways in *today's* realities.

This book also isn't about stress management. Undoubtedly, stress plays a significant role in your relationship to work and often exacerbates your dissatisfaction with it, but as counterintuitive as it sounds, you'll see that stress is also an important part of the solution to getting you out of the survival zone.

This isn't a book about burnout. While you will gain insights into how some of your most entrenched beliefs and practices may contribute to the problem, burnout is also a workplace systems issue and needs broader solutions. However, the tools I share will help you come back from burnout if that's where you find yourself heading.

Nor is this a book about self-care. Although the data clearly shows that people need more of this, the current approach to self-care is often too narrow to combat overwork and exhaustion in work and life. You will learn to expand that view; consider it "self-care 2.0" to broaden the impact of your practices.

Finally, workplace culture absolutely influences things, so it can't be discounted, but this book largely focuses on what you can do as an individual to change your relationship to work. After all, it is very challenging to single-handedly change your workplace culture. You do, however, have the most control over yourself, including your beliefs and behaviors and thus the actions you can take that make change possible.

This book does address all of these points, but they aren't the focus. As I learned from those everyday people who spent more time working in their stand-out zone, at the heart of changing our relationship to work is an energy issue. And I'm not just talking about managing your energy to get through the day. Many of you are doing that already, which may even be one of the reasons you feel stuck. I'm talking about cultivating and sustaining the kind of energy that allows you to work from the stand-out zone where you feel ready, willing, and wanting to take on the day ahead of you—adversity and all.

This aliveness, fueled by a sense of possibility, purposefulness, and ownership has a name that is rarely used but easily recognized in others and felt in ourselves. This take-on-the-day energy is called *vitality*.

You don't need to love your work, nor do you need to settle for dreading it, but you can feel a greater sense of aliveness engaging in it. *Dear Work* will help you establish a successful and healthy relationship with work by showing you how to reclaim your vitality, which together forms your Work Vitality Quotient. Strengthening that—so you *stand out without burning out* in the process—is the goal of this book.

In the pages ahead you will learn that when it comes to your vitality, the energy fueling it is influenced as much by your beliefs as it is by the actions you take to generate, replenish, and reinvigorate it. As such, we'll explore three categories of work relationship beliefs that have the biggest impact on boosting or depleting your Work Vitality Quotient:

- Your beliefs about *how you define and achieve success.*

- Your beliefs about *the nature and impact of stress.*

- Your beliefs about *the practices you employ to care for and replenish your energy.*

By addressing your beliefs and the strategies you can use to shift them, you'll see that being excellent in the work you do doesn't require being exhausted. You'll see that you can tip the balance away from overworking and under-living and that doing so doesn't equate to mediocrity in your success. You'll see that you can do so much more than simply survive the day and instead, rediscover the joy in it.

Make no mistake, in a world where the expectations keep growing, the lines between work and life keep blurring, and where hybrid and flexible work environments are the norm, raising your Work Vitality Quotient will be your distinct competitive advantage.

Warning: This Book Will Not Solve the Problem of Work

Before we dive in, I know I am supposed to tell you that after reading this book you will *finally* have the perfect solutions to your struggles. But I'm warning you now: that is an unrealistic expectation. In fact,

I'm going to suggest that part of the problem that contributes to people feeling locked in the survival zone is the temptation to look for a single, simple, permanent solution in a complex, dynamic, and changing world.

Try this perspective instead: changing your relationship to work starts by acknowledging that you will have busy periods that require one set of approaches and times that allow for more flexibility. Expect things will go off the rails and accept you'll get sucked into the survival zone. The key is not to get stuck there. Sometimes getting out will require applying a new strategy and other times you'll need to shift an old identity. *Dear Work* will help you recognize the difference and provide practical approaches—even when practiced imperfectly—to move you back into your stand-out zone. This last point is critical. No matter how frustrated, tired, or skeptical you feel, for change to happen, you must be willing to try new things and *do* things differently. As such, the recurring theme throughout this book is that everything counts. *Small-and-something* actions will always beat out *all-or-nothing* intentions.

When you view things this way, you'll see that cultivating your Work Vitality Quotient isn't a perfect solution or final destination; it's a process, and processes evolve as you evolve, and *that* is how enduring change occurs.

PART
ONE

Dear Vitality,

what exactly are you?

1

Your Work Vitality Quotient

FRAZZLED.
Fried.
Fed up.
Considering this is how many people describe feeling when it comes to work—and life for that matter—is it any wonder we seem to be experiencing a collective deficit of vitality these days? As someone who has a lot of conversations centered on these emotions and experiences, I've noticed an interesting trend. When I ask people how they *want to feel*, their answers are almost always the same. People describe wanting to feel *less* stressed, *less* tired, and *less* frustrated.

Sound familiar?

It is understandable that when you are in survival mode or feel on the brink of burnout, "less bad" is all that seems possible. The problem being, if less bad is your goal, then it is exactly what you get—*less of a thing you don't even want*—and that is a pretty low benchmark. Rest assured, if simply aiming to get through the day feeling less frazzled, fried, and fed up describes your desire right now, you are not alone. And while this experience is inarguably justified, it is also indicative of a mistake you may be making that is keeping you stuck in the survival zone. The good news is that shifting that benchmark is also the key to the solutions you are seeking to help move you into your stand-out zone.

Less Tired or More Alive?

I'm going to make a bold statement: I do not believe you are satisfied with just getting through the day. Nor do I believe you want to settle for feeling less stressed and less frustrated. I also suspect you are tired of feeling tired. You don't want to step back, and you don't want to lower the bar on your goals and desires. Instead, what I believe you *really want* is to rediscover your spark so you can:

- Feel more energized, fulfilled, and motivated both inside and outside of work.

- Align with your values and use your experience and expertise to make your highest contribution.

- Learn and grow in your career and possibly even have various careers.

- Have more fun and experience more freedom to live a full and meaningful life.

- Achieve your goals, give to others, and positively impact the world.

Can we just pause for a moment to appreciate how different the answers are when you shift the benchmark from what you don't want—or want to feel less of—to what you do want to feel more of? After all, what makes you feel less stressed is very different from what makes you feel most alive. And still, much of the traditional advice offered today emphasizes putting attention and efforts toward trying to *decrease exhaustion* when, as you've just seen, your efforts are better spent trying to *increase your energy*. These are vastly different approaches that result in significantly different outcomes and make boosting your Work Vitality Quotient unlike much of what is being proposed as solutions today.

To start, it is important to understand what vitality is and how it influences you and your relationship to work.

The Three Principles of Vitality

The root word of "vitality" is the Latin *vita*, which means life energy—the energy of aliveness. It is derived from physical *and* psychological energy. Physical vitality is described as feeling healthy, strong, and energetic. Mentally, emotionally, and spiritually, vitality describes feeling confident, resourceful, and that your actions have meaning and purpose. As such, your Work Vitality Quotient is boosted when your energy is directed toward people, projects, and pursuits that matter to you—in a way that is healthy for you.

Energy is a limited resource that must be replenished in order to be maintained. As vitality is energy based, you must protect it by investing in practices that nourish, refuel, and reinvigorate it. The key to vitality is that it is generated and sustained by using it *and* refueling it. Both are interconnected and equally necessary.

It's tempting to think that if your goal is to raise your Work Vitality Quotient, focusing solely on what you believe about work and what you do at work will produce the best results. But as you'll learn, this limited view is at the heart of our current vitality deficit. Your experience of vitality or the deficit of it will stretch beyond the borders of work. After all, you are part of a larger system that is influenced by various factors.

Instead, think of your vitality as stemming from three areas of your life: work, others, and self. *Work* includes the needs you must address in your job, career, or your life's work. *Others* includes the

Your Work
Vitality Quotient is
boosted when your
energy is directed
toward what matters
to you—in a way that
is healthy for you.

needs of people such as family, friends, and your broader community. And *Self* includes your own personal needs, goals, and desires. While all three areas are critical, rarely will you be able to give equal time, energy, and attention to each. However, when you overdraw on one or under-support another for too long, vitality becomes harder to find and impossible to sustain. Taking a more encompassing view allows you to better assess the full picture to discover opportunities and potential problems, and approach both in a more strategic way.

Pulling this all together, your *Work Vitality Quotient* is the combination of your mental, emotional, and physical energy fueling your capacity to:

- Chase down bold goals at *work*.

- Foster meaningful relationships with *others*.

- Pursue a fully lived, energized life that fulfills *you*.

The Business ROI of Vitality

Although this book focuses on your personal approach to work, the return on investment for businesses that develop and support the vitality of their employees is hard to dispute.

A growing body of research connects workplace vitality to increased levels of creativity, self-confidence, collaboration, adaptability, innovation, and performance. In my work in the field of leadership, I see people feeling more satisfied and balanced, as well as demonstrating higher levels of emotional intelligence and resilience. Perhaps most relevant today is that a stronger Work Vitality Quotient is associated with lowered burnout levels and better health and well-being indices.

According to McKinsey & Company's *Future of Work* report, the pandemic accelerated many existing trends and challenges.

Of particular relevance, it brought to the surface conversations about the human elements of work. Arianna Huffington, founder and CEO of Thrive Global, called the workplace fallout of the pandemic the Great Re-evaluation: "What people are resigning from is a culture of burnout and a broken definition of success." More than ever, people are re-examining their relationship with work, knowing that something needs to change.

While the benefits are compelling, raising your Work Vitality Quotient is not a one-stop-shop strategy. As such, if you are going to reclaim your vitality, you need to understand three important principles.

1 Vitality is personal.

2 Vitality is dynamic.

3 Vitality is intentional.

Vitality Is Personal

Perhaps the most important thing to remember when it comes to your Work Vitality Quotient is that there is no one way or right way to boost it. What generates vitality for you is often different from what ignites it in others. Some people feel most alive when they are creatively expressing themselves, others when they are conquering goals and testing their limits. For you, your aliveness may be ignited while advocating for change, teaching others, finding order and solutions, or creating something beautiful. The fact that vitality is personal and varied for everyone is what makes it so powerful.

Outside of work, experiences of aliveness might include listening to the birds with a coffee at sunrise, finishing a great workout, singing your heart out along with others at a concert, or listening to a detailed rundown of the day's events from your eight-year-old over dinner. It might be hearing a moving melody or taking in a beautiful landscape, piece of art, or architecture. Recognizing what vitality feels like to you and the types of experiences that generate it will help you cultivate more of it and sustain it in your work and life.

Take a moment to think about experiences at work, with others, and in your personal life where you felt most alive. If you are feeling exhausted, frustrated, overwhelmed, or sad, bringing an experience of aliveness to mind can feel challenging. If this is the case for you, I suggest looking through the photos on your phone for reminders. Or peruse your past calendar. Yes, you probably had many work meetings, but I suspect there are also entries associated with projects that brought forth the best of you or events that reinvigorated you. You can also ask other people about when they have seen you shine.

Identifying what ignites vitality for you requires exploring different paths, testing different options, pushing against norms, and getting uncomfortable. Don't judge yourself or hold yourself to others' expectations and opinions. Your vitality comes from within you, regardless of what others are doing, so there is no point in comparing yourself to others. One of the core reasons behind choosing to cultivate your vitality is to use it to make your most significant contribution to things that matter to you in life and work—so it only needs to be right for you.

Finally, vitality is rarely generated by trying to be less of you—or more of what you are not. Far too often, I speak with people who have been told that they are too driven, too competitive, too much of a perfectionist, too helpful, too empathetic, or too positive. Although strengths can become vices when overused, vitality is about embracing the whole of you. The authentic, imperfect, multidimensional, work-in-progress you.

Vitality Is Dynamic

Some days are just harder than others—even when you seem to be doing everything "right" by having dedicated self-care practices and doing work you care about. One of the biggest misconceptions about vitality is thinking that if you don't have it all the time, then you don't have it.

While consistently managing physical and psychological energy is essential, so is recognizing that vitality isn't a static state or a destination you get to, and then you're done. The feeling of vitality is dynamic in nature. It tends to be experienced intermittently, in varying intensities and frequencies, naturally ebbing and flowing throughout the day, over weeks, and over your lifetime. Add to this, the emotions we associate with vitality are also dynamic in range, including higher-energy emotions such as exhilaration, drive, and enthusiasm; and lower-energy emotions such as calm, connectedness, gratitude, and love.

Vitality's dynamism can also be attributed to the fact that it is influenced by both internal and external factors. First, it is experienced when your energy is directed toward things that are energizing and meaningful to you. In truth, some work is inherently meaningful, and some projects are more energizing. So, some days you will feel greater levels of vitality than others. This is natural.

Next, vitality is generated from energy and all energy sources need to be replenished to be sustained. This is non-negotiable. Depending on the demands you face, plus the time you can dedicate to rest and recovery, means some days your energy resources will understandably be running low.

Finally, we all face times of heightened stress and adversity which will inevitably impact our sense of vitality. Examples of adversity may include social injustices, financial stress, an unexpected health diagnosis, or losing a job or an important relationship—anything that causes grief. Although we wouldn't expect people to feel enthusiastic and vibrant under these circumstances, vitality is often experienced as a result of stress, struggle, or tragedy.

Take, for example, Mothers Against Drunk Driving, founded by Candace Lightner after her thirteen-year-old daughter was killed by a drunk driver. Or Black Lives Matter, founded by three Black women organizers—Alicia Garza, Patrisse Cullors, and Opal Tometi—

The power of
vitality is that it
can be experienced
in many ways,
cultivated through
different practices,
and used in
different formats.

---

in response to the acquittal in the fatal shooting of seventeen-year-old Trayvon Martin. Many volunteers at and donors to foundations and associations have been personally affected by trying and tragic events.

Although I don't know if the specific people referenced above feel a sense of vitality doing their work, what I do know from the data, the countless stories I heard while researching for this book, including my own experience with grief, is that vitality can take different forms. Seeing loss and adversity as a conduit for change and the opportunity to be of service can ignite an enduring spark that, while challenging, is also energizing.

In early 2021, I was on a video call with my client Dale. After describing the devastating effect of the pandemic on his team and him personally, he explained how it also allowed him to "reimagine the future of learning" for his company. Without negating the challenges, he lit up with vibrance and vigor as he talked about how he was embracing this time of great upheaval and using its momentum to make important changes that had been sitting on the backburner for far too long. Sometimes it's in the contrast between positive and negative experiences that vitality is most potently experienced.

At the end of my call with Dale, I felt inspired to reimagine my future. That is the other power of vitality: not only is it noticeable, but it's also contagious—and not just person-to-person, but within organizations as well. With burnout levels so high, flexible working models still being tested, and an urgent focus on employee retention, diversity, inclusion, and attracting and keeping younger generations of people—a vitality-infused culture gives your organization a powerful edge.

Vitality Is Intentional

Just as we need oxygen, water, and sleep to stay alive, having a sense of agency over our lives is key to making us *feel* alive. Agency is the belief that you have the power to act in a way that will influence your environment and desired outcomes. The opposite of agency is when you feel helpless, hopeless, and at the mercy of circumstance. With this definition in mind, recognize that vitality is not reserved for the fortunate few whose career and life are going as planned. Everyone experiences vitality; however, cultivating enduring vitality rarely happens by accident—it requires intentional time, attention, and action.

When it comes to raising your Work Vitality Quotient, you already know that directing your energy toward meaningful work is key. The challenge is that people often believe it is the role of their leader or company to give them meaningful work, motivate them, and ensure they feel energized. This is where people inadvertently surrender their sense of agency. In a study conducted at the University of California, Berkeley, researchers found that when people described work they found invigorating and meaningful, rarely did they mention it having anything to do with their organization or manager. However, when people described their work as meaningless and, in turn, vitality depleting, it was almost exclusively related to the organization or the lack of support and clarity from their managers.

Of course, anyone who has ever worked for a toxic boss or within a crisis-driven organization that shifts directions and priorities in head-spinning ways knows that pursuing, let alone completing, meaningful work can be challenging even on the best days. Feeling powerless to change anything makes the idea of raising your Work Vitality Quotient feel impossible.

But as you'll see throughout this book, vitality is as much about your perspective as it is about your circumstances. Consider the difference between the following questions: "Did you feel a sense of vitality at work today?" And the same question framed differently: "Did *you do your best* to cultivate a sense of vitality in your work today?"

The second question is an agency-creating question. It shifts the focus internally to what you are doing for yourself, making you far more likely to focus on the actions you can take versus the external

Vitality is as much
about your perspective
as it is about your
circumstances.

circumstances that may or may not have contributed to feeling a sense of vitality.

Agency empowers you to say no to unrealistic demands and yes to healthy boundaries so you and others can function at your highest capabilities. It helps you to stop, reflect, and reset even when everyone else seems to be running to check that where you're headed still makes sense. To look inside and investigate if your pride, outdated beliefs, limiting stories, or a gap in your skill set are contributing to your depleted vitality—and to courageously acknowledge and choose to change them when they are.

While it is undeniable that your circumstances influence vitality, raising your Work Vitality Quotient must be approached as an intentional personal pursuit, not one where you wait for people, timing, or circumstances to create it for you.

As you go through this book, keep each of these principles in mind, as they will underscore the practices of how to raise *your* Work Vitality Quotient. But before we move on, there are three emotions that provoke a strong sense of aliveness but are not the same as vitality. Clarifying each will help ensure your goals and actions are channeled in the most strategic and meaningful way.

Happiness

While happiness—or specifically, the excitement we associate with happiness from pleasurable experiences—is a positive emotion that can arouse a sense of aliveness, it tends to be short-lived and often comes from external inputs. For example, you might get some great feedback in the morning from a client and be happy and then get a text from your soon-to-be ex-spouse, and suddenly your feeling of happiness is gone.

In contrast, vitality is derived from positive energy and is more enduring. It tends to be generated internally and makes you feel capable, purposeful, and resourceful to face whatever circumstances come up. In other words, you can feel frustrated and unhappy with your circumstances and still feel strong and energized to deal with them.

Passion
· · · · · · · · ·

You undoubtedly feel alive when pursuing things that you are passionate about. However, to generate vitality requires also doing things you may not feel passionate about but that are important. For example, staying hydrated or getting sleep so that you have the healthy, positive energy you need to pursue your passions.

On the one hand, passion can become very singular in nature. When passion becomes so intense that it excludes giving attention to other areas of life, this results in an unbalanced and unhealthy lifestyle. Vitality, on the other hand, reflects living in a healthy way and is best sustained by holistically addressing the needs of work, others, and self.

Anger
· · · · · · ·

The experience of feeling alive can come from anger, but the end goal of the emotion generated matters. Anger is an intense negative emotion; as such, the energy generated from anger has a fast burn rate when it comes to motivation. Conversely, vitality is energy that generates positive emotions and provides enduring motivation.

When anger results in cynicism, hate, or harm, that is not vitality. However, using anger to fuel possibility and purpose to drive positive and productive change is how you transform the energy generated by anger into the aliveness of vitality.

2

The Science of Your
Work Vitality

PAUSE for a moment and reflect on this question: what is one strategy that, if you were to put into practice today, would have you firing on all cylinders to take on the challenges you'll inevitably face in the week ahead? I've asked hundreds of people this question and have never heard anyone say, "You know, I can't think of a single thing." So, I am quite confident that you too have an answer.

The issue isn't that you don't know what to do and are in desperate need of more strategies; the problem is that those strategies feel impossible to apply in exactly the moments when you know they would be most helpful.

Consider the last time you left a conference, saw a post, read a book, or listened to a podcast feeling inspired to make changes. Maybe you wrote down your goal, downloaded a tracking app, and put together your plan to employ a new strategy. You re-entered reality with the absolute best of intentions only to be hit by the same old busyness. The next thing you knew, you abandoned your plan, your new strategy vaporized, and you were back to the old habit, which just so happened to be the same one you were trying to change.

In the aftermath of a failed attempt to change, most of us do one or more of the following: We blame and beat ourselves up for not having enough willpower or discipline to follow through and make the change. We blame our circumstances, and usually others, for making it impossible to enact our plan. Or we just assume the strategy we chose doesn't work and we continue our endless search for the magic bullet that does.

While this explanation is both typical and understandable, it is based on a faulty assumption—you assumed logic would prevail in the moment you needed to put your new strategy to work. After all, as a sensible, logical person, you know what is best for you and presume you'll make decisions accordingly. The challenge with this assumption is that especially in stress-invoking situations, your brain is designed for emotional reasoning, *not* logical thought, to drive your decision making. As you'll learn, this is why you are naturally biased to do what is easiest (employ your old habits) versus what is best for you (enact your new habit).

When you understand your brain's design, much of the mystery behind why you do what you do, or perhaps more to the point, why you don't do the things you know you should, can be explained. Armed with these insights, you can more effectively apply the strategies that will strengthen your Work Vitality Quotient instead of sinking energy into a fight against the very way your brain works.

Your Brain Wants Comfort

Fundamentally, the human brain is optimized to prioritize survival and desire comfort. As a result, it will typically take the safest path of least resistance for the most immediate reward. After all, its primary goal is to keep you alive, but that is much different from doing things that make you feel alive.

This prioritization framework explains why your brain will opt for feeling better over being better without intentional intervention. In other words, what you *want to do* and what is *best for you to do* frequently conflict. This tug-of-war, which is happening all the time, is why your impulse is to mindlessly reach for your phone 400 times an hour when working on something difficult or feeling overwhelmed, instead of mindfully spending two minutes taking deep breaths and grounding yourself. Logically, you know the latter is a better way to manage energy and buffer the impact of stress. But looking at a phone feels better in the moment. It takes minimal effort, gives you a little dopamine boost in anticipation of seeing something new in your feed, and allows you to avoid tasks or problems you don't want to think about.

Here's the thing: many of our choices and habits may not be harmful, but they may be less uplifting and revitalizing than other choices could be. Case in point, when we feel as if we're drowning in the survival zone, our natural tendency is to reach for outlets that help us feel less exhausted (feel better) rather than taking the actions to feel more energized (be better).

Your Brain Needs Challenge

While your brain naturally prioritizes safety, and desires comfort, predictability, and immediate happiness, it also thrives on *challenge*.

Your Brain Wants Comfort	Your Brain Needs Challenge
Safety	Learning
Happiness	Meaning
Predictability	Change
Effortlessness	Mindfulness
Instant gratification	Sustainable fulfillment

Learning about the world, connecting to a sense of meaning, embracing change and uncertainty, being mindful with your attention, and seeking deep, lasting fulfillment are not only experiences that make you feel alive but are how you get the best from your brain as well. Simply put, your brain wants comfort but it needs challenge.

When it comes to a healthy brain, how extensively connected your various brain regions are, how strong the connections, and how actively new connections are made are all important factors that contribute to building what is known as your brain's cognitive reserve. The truth is that your brain is malleable and can change through a process called brain plasticity. What prompts such a malleable, healthy, robustly interconnected neural network? You guessed it, getting outside your comfort zone.

By engaging in challenging activities and diverse experiences— especially ones that require moving your body and involve multiple senses at once, you can change your brain and add to this reserve. Think of all these neural connections as your brain's back-up system for accessing your experiences, expertise, and memories. If one link fails or becomes damaged, the brain can create and utilize previously established connections to tap into this information. The broader your neural network system, the more efficient and creatively you can gain access to that information to flexibly respond and engage with the world.

Add to this, your brain is biased for vitality. When you engage in activities that make you feel alive, that are meaningful, energizing, and draw on your strengths, your brain more readily builds denser connections and stronger networks, which is also why you tend to experience the greatest learning, growth, and resilience when engaging in these activities.

It's important to acknowledge that what constitutes a challenge and getting outside one's comfort zone may differ from one person to the next. For some, what's challenging is sticking to a routine and getting off the couch, whether that's to exercise or go out with friends. For others, being surrounded by people, constantly being

Your brain *wants* comfort, but it *needs* challenge.

on the move, and striving for the next big thing is most comfortable, but relaxing and being alone is like having teeth pulled without novocaine.

What is inarguable is that taking the path of least resistance rarely leads to the achievement of bold goals and deep bonds with others. Nor does it lend itself to a full life that includes facing adversity and finding joy. Hence *vitality and challenge go hand in hand.*

To be clear, comfort, ease, and happiness are not bad or wrong. Sometimes a quick shot of immediate reward is exactly what we need to shift moods. Some of our most creative ideas come from allowing our brains to go offline and our bodies to slow down. Mastery of skills comes from practicing the same thing over and over so we can do it automatically and with greater ease. Happiness and lightheartedness allow us to laugh, which floods our system with feel-good chemicals, strengthens our immune response, eases anxiety, and buffers us from life's hardships. It isn't an either-or situation; it is both—your brain needs both comfort and challenge.

What matters is mindfully choosing which actions are in service of cultivating vitality instead of mindlessly acquiescing to what feels easiest in the moment. Finding this balance is how you boost your Work Vitality Quotient and flourish in your stand-out zone.

To recognize when your brain is trying to negotiate you out of what's best and into what's easiest, you need to understand the influence of some key brain players: the prefrontal cortex, the amygdala and hippocampus, and the hormone cortisol.

The Prefrontal Cortex

The prefrontal cortex has a critical role in cultivating and sustaining your Work Vitality Quotient. Anytime you've been faced with adversity and adjusted your approach in search of opportunities rather than getting stuck by obstacles, you've engaged your prefrontal cortex.

It is responsible for reflective and complex thought, weighing out different options, and considering alternative viewpoints to make decisions. As such, it plays a critical role in regulating your emotional impulses. It helps you to stay connected to future consequences and the bigger picture, including the values you associate with strengthening your Work Vitality Quotient.

When you're firing on all cylinders, the prefrontal cortex can think strategically, prioritize appropriately, and execute effectively, which are key descriptors of what it means to work in your stand-out zone. However, for all of the amazing things it does, this bit of gray matter also has its limitations.

First and foremost, it has limited bandwidth and fatigues with use. If you've ever spent the day on never-ending video calls, barely leaving your chair, only to feel like you've run a marathon at the end of it all, you can appreciate how energy-intensive prefrontal cortex work can be. The more tired you are, the less vigilant and more distracted it becomes, the more shortcuts it looks for, and the less efficiently it performs. Simply put, when you overtax your prefrontal cortex, the more it will bias you to what is safe and easiest in the moment, even if it ends up pushing you into the survival zone in the long run. To keep on working in the stand-out zone, your prefrontal cortex needs dedicated periods of rest to replenish its capacity.

Perhaps its most notable limitation, though, is that the prefrontal cortex can be overpowered by your limbic system, particularly the amygdala.

The Amygdala, the Hippocampus, and Cortisol

If you've ever walked by a perfume counter, caught the faintest whisp of the fragrance your first crush in high school wore, and found yourself instantly transported back in time, then you've experienced the influence of the brain's limbic system. While distinct from your prefrontal cortex, the various parts of your brain are connected and work together.

The limbic system plays a central role in emotional processing and regulation, memory, and motivating the behaviors needed for survival. This includes controlling your stress responses as well as behaviors associated with reproduction, feeding, and nurturing. In the simplest terms, the limbic system aims to keep you physically and psychologically safe.

The amygdala and the hippocampus are two major components of the limbic system. The amygdala is responsible for emotional processing, and the hippocampus is the brain's main long-term memory system. Both are closely connected to smell, one of the most rudimentary survival senses. And so, when the heady drift of CK One tickles your nostrils, it is the amygdala and hippocampus, working in concert, that trigger the intense emotion and associated memories.

Amygdala

Here is where things get interesting. If moments later you also detected the fragrance Biff, the high school bully, wore, your amygdala would instantly prioritize that scent above your crush's CK One, putting you on high alert—as if Biff the bully were standing right in front of you. Even though *logically* you would know they weren't, your amygdala would have already sounded the alarm, before your prefrontal cortex had time to remind you that you haven't seen Biff in over twenty years. This is why, when it comes to negative experiences, the amygdala (and our emotions) get the upper hand in driving your decisions and associated behaviors. After all, protecting yourself from a bully is more important to your safety and survival than attracting your crush's attention.

Unlike the prefrontal cortex, which tends to fatigue with use, the amygdala gets stronger and increasingly sensitive the more it is activated. Self-protection is paramount to the amygdala, so it makes sense that not all emotions get the same attention. In fact, two-thirds of the amygdala's neurons are dedicated to detecting negative stimuli. As a result, you feel the onset of negative emotions faster, more fiercely, and for longer than positive ones. This propensity for negative emotions to get more attention is known as the brain's negativity bias, and while useful in motivating you toward comfort and safety, it can be detrimental if left unchecked.

Take digital communication or working in virtual environments as examples. When there is an absence of information, your brain's natural inclination is to fill that unknown with contextual information that leans toward the worst-case scenario. This explains why digital communications tend to be interpreted more negatively without the context of body language and tone. We've all had an experience where a loved one has sent us a "call me" text, to which our brain jumps to a worst-case scenario only to be met with some humdrum question upon calling back.

The negativity bias is even more pronounced when engaging with someone whom you perceive as having more authority, such as your boss. After all, staying in the good graces of someone who has the power or influence to impact your future is the safest thing you can do, which is why a leader's actions, especially when it comes to how they approach success, deal with stress, and practice rest, have such an influential effect on workplace culture. The brain's negativity bias is designed to help you be extra vigilant to signs that this security is at stake and take actions to re-establish it as quickly as possible. As a result, the old adage of "no news is good news" does not hold up from a neurological perspective, especially when that "no news" is coming from a boss whom, for example, you are worried doesn't trust you are working hard when remote. With your brain's negativity bias, no news gets interpreted as bad news.

Hippocampus

Your nostalgia at smelling a scent you associate with the memory of your first crush that is decades old highlights the close connection between emotion and memory. The role of the hippocampus is

In survival mode
we mistakenly
look for ways to feel
less exhausted
rather than more
energized.

central to encoding emotional context to your experiences and is critical in learning, emotional responses, as well as memory formation and storage. As such, one of its jobs is prioritization, informing how important something is and how urgently you need to respond to it.

Like the amygdala, the hippocampus prioritizes intense, novel, and negative emotions and experiences and stores them as memories more quickly, making them easily accessible to retrieve as compared to positive or normal, everyday experiences.

Let's test this for a moment: think back to a childhood moment when you felt proud and one when you felt embarrassed. Which most readily comes to mind? Chances are you remember with more vivid detail the embarrassing situation.

Alternatively, when it comes to positive emotions and experiences, they tend to pass through both, quickly fading from your amygdala's attention and hippocampus's memory. That is, unless you deliberately direct and hold your attention to focus on positive emotions. As you'll learn, being mindful with your attention and emotions is critical to sustainably strengthening your Work Vitality Quotient.

Cortisol

The final important element of your physiology as it relates to the Work Vitality Quotient is cortisol, which also happens to be the most recognized of the stress hormones. While it often gets a bad rap, cortisol is an important, beneficial, and naturally occurring hormone essential to your day-to-day functioning, including helping you get moving in the morning and wind down in the evening.

When released in response to stress, cortisol helps your brain and body prepare to meet short-term demands—again, essential and beneficial. However, when the body's natural stress response doesn't run through its needed cycle, which allows cortisol levels to rise and then return to their natural baseline circulating levels, the often-cited wear-and-tear effects of stress occur.

When cortisol levels cease to naturally fluctuate and remain steady in your system, it is known as dysregulation. The two parts

of the brain that are most adversely affected by cortisol dysregulation are the hippocampus and prefrontal cortex, resulting in,
among other things, decreased emotional regulation, learning, and
efficiency.

Why Even the Best Strategies Are So Hard to Apply

It's time to pull this all together and apply what you've learned
about the brain to better understand why even the best and most
logical strategies are hard to apply in the moments they would be
most helpful. Let's pretend you have a goal of getting more sleep by
using a strategy to stop working in the evenings. I'm going to invite
you to think about the last time you felt totally overwhelmed as you
found yourself working much later into the night than intended.
Now imagine a loved one suggesting you shut it down. Chances
are your response would go something like: "You don't understand.
I can't. I have to keep working—there is too much to do, and people
are counting on me!"

Even before your loved one tentatively cleared their throat and
plucked up their courage to suggest a full night's sleep might help
you gain perspective, your cortisol-sensitive hippocampus had
already mistakenly started overcoding everything as urgent and
important. This meant your ability to prioritize was diminished—
everything seemed top priority and needed to be done yesterday—so
of course you believed you couldn't stop.

Your tenacious amygdala, however, dutifully kept up with its job
of sounding the alarm while simultaneously taking the reins from
the prefrontal cortex. Your negativity bias kicked in and locked in
on the worst-case scenario, making you feel sure that if you stopped
working, everything would fall apart.

Your overtaxed prefrontal cortex (which, let's face it, had called
it quits shortly after your all-too-brief dinner break) which was
already struggling to work efficiently, is now disconnected from the

big picture and future consequences. Influenced by the amygdala and hippocampus, your brain is now negotiating you toward your old ways with all-or-nothing thinking making you believe there is no other option than to dig deeper, push harder, and work longer. This short-sighted, self-protective strategy sinks you deeper into the survival zone. The same zone you originally wanted to escape, which motivated the strategy you are now overriding.

While I suspect we've all been there in some form at least once, you've probably also had times where you've listened to your loved one, taken a break, and then come back to work a few hours, a day, a weekend later with a different outlook. With a rested brain, you now see that perhaps not *everything* is urgent, the world may not *fall apart*, and there are some *options* on how to move things forward in a way that doesn't require late nights that deprioritize your health and personal needs. You question how you didn't see this before.

If, at this point, you are tempted to conclude from all this that your brain is working against you and will thwart your efforts to work in vitality-enhancing ways—resist! You don't need to fight your brain. It isn't trying to screw you over. It's simply trying to keep you safe and comfortable, which it is designed to do.

When you learn to recognize the red flag signals of the survival zone, which you'll do in the next chapter, you can reverse engineer actions to shift decision making from the amygdala to the prefrontal cortex and intentionally take steps to get you back to working from your stand-out zone. Even better, you can pre-emptively go upstream from these late-night moments when you will almost certainly feel overwhelmed and stuck in an all-or-nothing, trade-off mindset and incorporate practices that decrease the chance of being there in the first place. Boosting your Work Vitality Quotient becomes more accessible when you're aware of your brain's instincts and can apply strategies in a brain-savvy way. One in particular that we'll consistently come back to is tapping into your brain's natural propensity for wonder.

Designed for Worry—and Wonder
. . . .

Along with the negatively biased worry circuits designed to keep you safe, your brain is also wired for a sense of wonder about the world. This "wonder circuitry" is known as the seeking system. In his book *Alive at Work*, Dan Cable puts it like this: "Seeking systems create the natural impulse to explore our worlds, learn about our environments, and extract meaning from our circumstances... When our seeking system is activated, we feel more motivated, purposeful, and zestful. We feel more alive."

One of the easiest ways to activate your wonder circuitry is by asking yourself questions that challenge your assumptions, expand your possibilities, and purposefully connect you to what matters most. Not only do questions help re-engage your prefrontal cortex, but they also instill a sense of agency, empowering you to experiment with the approaches and the beliefs you hold about your circumstances and how you get things done. Throughout this book, you will see time and again the power and utilization of your wonder circuitry in the process of cultivating of your Work Vitality Quotient.

3

Establishing Your Key
Vitality Indicators

IT WAS my turn to pick the movie. For the past couple of months, my husband and I had been practicing an end-of-weekend wind-down routine, which included watching a show together before bed. There were three rules to this routine: it started at eight o'clock; it was to be distraction-free, meaning no phones, no work; and whoever's week it was to choose the show must have made their choice *before* the start time. This last rule was a recent add after multiple Sunday nights were spent endlessly scrolling to find something we were both in the mood to watch. Inevitably, the decision would be made by one of us shoving the remote toward the other saying, "Whatever, I don't care, you pick." Not the most relaxing start to a wind-down routine. On this Sunday evening, my computer was still open, papers surrounded me, I had not yet fulfilled my movie-picking duties, and it was 7:59 p.m.

Right on time, my husband walked into the living room expectantly asking what we'd be watching. Recognizing the scene, he sighed and said, "So, no movie tonight, I guess?" I'd be lying if I said that this was the first Sunday night that something like this had happened. To make matters worse, earlier that weekend, we'd argued after I'd suggested we cut an upcoming vacation short so that I could get a head start on a project.

I'd genuinely intended to relax with my husband and, truthfully, I really needed it. I was on the last leg of a busy speaking season and had spent the entire month trying to get rid of a persistent cold that left me feeling like a zombie. I was running on fumes and had been for a while, so I was increasingly finding myself in a generally grumpy, impatient, and distracted state. I'd been working all weekend on a huge client project. Even though my brain was exhausted, something was off with the project, and I thought I could figure it out if I could just get a couple more hours in.

As I silently contemplated packing it all up for the night or working through movie time, I had an idea. Excitedly I told my husband, "No TV tonight, something better!" Skeptically, he sat down beside me as I slid a copy of the self-assessment I'd been working on across the coffee table toward him. "You can assess me!"

In hindsight, I realize that assessing your spouse on their level of emotional intelligence is probably not more fun than watching a riveting episode of *Dateline* on a Sunday night. But I was confident I had a good idea of the feedback he'd share. He'd say that I'm not always the best listener. I tend to want to solve problems too quickly. Although it wasn't on the assessment, it would be fair if he gave me a failing grade on my ability to remember his very detailed dishwasher-loading preferences. But he knew me. He knew how much I valued our relationship and how invested I was in my work. Having him assess me seemed like a chance to get real insight and to walk my talk. Not to mention the bonus of getting to share the experience with my audience the next day.

His response, however, wasn't to grab a pen and start. Instead, he slid the assessment back across the coffee table, shaking his head and saying, "No."

Before I could argue, he said, "I know you love what you do..." and looking right at me without any blame or judgment in his voice, he calmly said, "It just means I don't always get the best of you." I was crushed. I wanted to defend myself but stopped. He was right. I knew that the people who deserved the best of me, who loved and supported me, and (it's not a stretch to say) who at times put up with me—weren't getting the best of me. What they were getting was the leftover me. And as I sat there feeling ashamed, I realized I wasn't getting the best of me either.

The Leftover-You Cycle

It's natural and expected to find yourself oscillating between highly stressful periods where a significant amount of your time, attention, and energy goes into work. I have busy speaking seasons where I travel extensively. Other times I find myself needing to put in long days to meet a deadline for a writing or client project. Maybe for you, it's in the lead-up to a major product launch, closing a potentially business-altering contract, or fiscal year-end. And, of course, there are also times when multiple deadlines converge, life outside of work goes off the rails, or unexpected crises emerge (pandemic, anyone?). The challenge is that although these high-intensity periods are meant to be temporary, you keep working in high-intensity ways even after the demanding period has passed. To compensate, you try to take a long weekend here and there, but always keeping an eye on work. You come back to work feeling "less stressed" and "less tired" and consider that good enough.

Most people don't realize that the longer you stay in this cycle, the more you inadvertently lower the bar—mentally, emotionally, and physically—on what counts as feeling "good." Little by little, *survival mode just becomes normal mode.*

If this describes you, welcome to your humanness in action. In general, we humans are not very good at recognizing the impact fatigue has on us personally or on our performance. This isn't a flaw of human nature; it is part of the powerful way we learn to adapt with resilience to changing and challenging situations.

Adjusting to Running on Fumes
. . . .

In one telling sleep study, researchers put study participants on a fourteen-day sleep restriction regimen. The researchers were interested in measuring two things: how sleep deprivation impacted moods and performance, and how people's perception of sleep deprivation changed over time. Participants were allowed six hours of sleep a night. I'll pause there as I suspect many of you who are reading this would not consider six hours of sleep a night a "restricted regimen." However, there are dozens upon dozens of studies showing that adults require, on average, seven to nine hours of sleep for maximal health.

The study subjects would assess their moods daily. They would also participate in performance-focused physical and mental tasks. As expected, the more one's sleep debt accumulated, the more errors and lapses in judgment a person made. Here is the fascinating part: for the first few days, people recorded increasingly feeling the effects of being tired, recognizing how it impacted their mood, energy, and behavior. They also accurately assessed the negative impact their fatigue was having on their performance.

But by day seven, people were far less aware of how their lack of sleep was impacting them, even while their moods noticeably changed. In fact, most reported that they had begun to feel better, believing it was because they were getting used to sleeping less. They significantly underestimated the impact their fatigue was having on performance as well, believing their accuracy and efficiency had leveled out even though they continued to decline.

How is this possible? One explanation is that when participants were assessing how tired they felt, they used a renormalization process. Each day the participants assessed their level of fatigue. You'd think they'd be making that comparison based on what they felt like at their best. But instead, people tended to unknowingly compare how they felt in that moment to how they generally felt in the days before. In the initial days of the study the differences were

Are the people
that deserve the best
of you getting it,
or are they getting
the leftover you?

---

significant as the research participants compared themselves to what it felt like to be fully rested. But as the days went on it became harder to remember what they felt like before the experiment. This meant that the participants used fatigue as their comparative benchmark. After five to seven days, the differences in their unrested state were smaller and less discernible. While they were getting used to *feeling* less rested, they started to mistake feeling "less bad" as "things getting better."

While this process is critical to your ability to adapt and get through difficult situations, it is also a key culprit in how survival mode becomes everyday mode. When you assess your physical, mental, and emotional state, you compare how you feel today to how you felt yesterday; you can quickly forget how you felt even five days earlier, and especially what it felt like to be at your best. This is even more pronounced when you neglect to take breaks and vacations, which not only allow you to recharge but help you reset your benchmark of feeling rested and energized.

Who hasn't experienced an unexpectedly refreshing weekend and said, "Wow, I didn't realize how much I needed that"? Unfortunately, it is not until we feel good that we realize just how bad we felt before.

Add to this, your brain's design means you are far less effective at recalling in detail positive experiences compared to negative ones. As such, having a stand-out zone "best of me" benchmark is needed to monitor and compare yourself against accurately. Enter Key Vitality Indicators.

Key Vitality Indicators

One of the most influential thinkers on modern management, Peter Drucker, famously said, "What is measured is managed, and what is managed gets improved." This premise is the basis of Key Performance Indicators (KPIs). KPIs allow organizations to track progress toward a set of performance objectives and notice trends and deviations. They help everyone stay on the same page while providing a snapshot of a business's overall health.

This idea isn't just a business concept anymore. If you own a fitness tracker, then chances are good you regularly monitor KPIs to see how much sleep you got, how many steps you took, and how often you stood. If you use it with exercise, you likely track your workouts, heart rate, and calories.

You can apply the same principle when exploring how to manage your energy using *Key Vitality Indicators* (KVIs). Your KVIs are a set of personal self-monitoring vitality indicators—or benchmarks—representing what it feels like to be firing on all cylinders in your stand-out zone. Descriptions like mentally creative, emotionally calm, and physically rested are examples of KVIs. The goal of establishing your KVIs is to help you understand how your mental, emotional, and physical energy levels are trending in relation to your benchmarks to help you work in your stand-out zone.

A significant difference between performance indicators and vitality indicators is that performance is a static benchmark to measure against; you are on track or off track. Vitality is dynamic and so are your energy sources that feed it. As such, you should expect your energy levels to ebb and flow throughout the day. For example, you won't always feel creative, but when you notice yourself moving further from this mental energy KVI, you can take strategic actions to help you get back to it or at least feel more of it.

KVIs build awareness by helping you pay attention to and understand what your energy is communicating to you. From this, you can learn to recognize the difference between your brain's resistance to doing hard things in which you can keep drawing on available energy and when you are overdrawing on your resources and need rest.

Finally, it's important to recognize that your KVIs may also change depending on context. What makes you feel most alive at work may be different than what helps you give your best at home.

Your Key Vitality
Indicators represent
you in your
stand-out zone and
provide benchmarks
to show you how
your mental, emotional,
and physical energy
sources are trending.

Establishing Your KVIs
. . . .

Establishing KVIs that are representative of you begins with a simple reflection. If you've never done something like this before, start by simply paying attention to your energy over the course of the week—tracking the highs and lows, what contributes to energy boosts and what doesn't. Notice what is happening in your body, to your thinking, and with your emotions. With this insight, you can establish your KVIs.

Step #1: Reflect On You in Your Stand-Out Zone

Reflect on what it feels like when you're working from your stand-out zone—where you feel capable of bringing your best, most energized self in the healthiest and most fulfilling way. With this in mind, record your responses to the following questions:

- How would you describe feeling mentally, emotionally, and physically?

- What types of thoughts do you have, perspectives do you take, and behaviors and reactions do you exhibit when faced with difficult or stressful situations?

- What are the potential differences in your answers when you reflect on your personal life outside of work?

For example, when you are firing on all cylinders from your stand-out zone, perhaps you feel clear-minded, patient, able to untangle complex problems, and are more willing to brush off the little things and feel more grateful for the important things. Maybe you stay curious and ask more questions, think more strategically, and articulate your thoughts and expectations more influentially.

Personally, when I'm in my stand-out zone at work, I am focused and flexible in how I get things done. I am a better listener and feel full of ideas and excitement about the future. At home, I tend to be much more present, supportive, and fun. I also find myself laughing a lot and prioritizing things that feed my energy and strengthen my health.

Step #2: Identify and Organize Your Stand-Out Zone Descriptors

Review your reflections in step one, and write down several single-word descriptors that summarize what it feels like when you are in your stand-out zone.

An important note as you work through this exercise: don't worry about finding the perfect descriptors or if you have them in the right categories. The goal is to build your awareness and have a set of indicators that represent you.

Organize your single-word descriptors into three categories: mental energy, emotional energy, and physical energy. Remember, you can change these at any time. Examples of single-word descriptors include:

- **Mental energy:** Focused, creative, productive, agile, strategic, decisive

- **Emotional energy:** Open, positive, motivated, curious, engaged, compassionate, calm, excited, fulfilled, committed, empathetic, confident

- **Physical energy:** Rested, strong, ready, hyped, healthy, refreshed, relaxed, restored, peppy, energized

Step #3: Select Your Stand-Out Zone KVIs

From your lists, choose the most important stand-out zone "indicators" to help you monitor each energy source at work and at home. To do this, choose one word from each energy source category that feels most like an amplifier of stand-out zone behaviors. In other words, when you feel this way, you do everything better. For example, the mental energy KVI that is most important to me at work is *focus*. When I'm focused, I work more strategically and productively. I can better prioritize tasks and I'm less likely to overcommit myself.

However, at home my mental energy KVI is being *present*. When I am present, I tend to be very deliberate with my attention and am better at listening and more aware of how my emotions and moods impact my actions. In summary, my work KVIs include:

- **Mental KVI:** *Focus*

- **Emotional KVI:** *Open*

- **Physical KVI:** *Energized*

Once you have examples of what each of your energy source KVIs looks like in action, you will be able to better assess how each trend over time—and ensure you don't shortchange yourself on the activities that protect, nourish, replenish, and reinvigorate your sense of vitality.

Establishing Your Red Flags

As powerful as your stand-out zone energy KVIs are, you also have to watch the renormalization effect, which makes gradual dips and negative trends harder to spot in a timely way. You address this by working with your brain's design and simply contrasting your KVIs with survival zone red flags—indicators of when you move away from your stand-out zone and into the survival zone. As your brain is inherently wired to be more aware of danger signals, having clear cautionary indicators will help you notice when you're over-drawing on your energy resources. To do this, simply repeat the first set of stand-out zone reflections, but this time for the survival zone.

Step #1: Reflect On You in Your Survival Zone

Reflect on what it feels like when you're running on fumes and working from the survival zone. With this in mind, record your responses to the following questions:

- How would you describe feeling mentally, emotionally, and physically?

- What types of thoughts do you have, perspectives do you take, and behaviors and reactions do you exhibit when faced with difficult or stressful situations?

- What are the potential differences in your answers when you reflect on your personal life outside of work?

A respondent to one survey I conducted described that the more maxed out he feels, the more impatient he becomes and the quicker he is to snap at his kids. In meetings, he's often more abrupt and is much more likely to fire off frustrated emails late into the evenings, even when he knows it will probably only make things worse. Many people report being unable to concentrate, thinking more negatively, being less empathetic, and feeling more irritable. Others describe oscillating between crushing it and crashing so they feel like they are running around frantically to get everything done to lethargically lying on the couch, binge-watching TV for hours. Physical energy red flags might include sleep disruption, muscle aches and tension, weight gain, or digestion issues. Most concerning is when responses shift into unhealthy coping strategies, such as excessive drinking, eating, shopping, gambling, or drug use.

Even the little things can be signs of survival mode, like being more distracted, forgetful, clumsier, or moodier. A few of my red flags include being less clear with my expectations and then (unfairly) expecting people to read my mind and know what I need. I make more careless mistakes. I overcommit myself at work and cancel commitments in my personal life. I take things more personally, especially things that usually make me laugh. Non-work tasks get pushed to the backburner until the last possible moment or they become an emergency. One of my most telling survival zone red flags, which I am embarrassed to admit, is when I take on a helpless or victim mindset causing me to compare, complain, and waste time commiserating instead of taking action to address things.

Step #2: Identify Your Red Flags

From your reflections, choose the most representative survival zone red flag indicators for each category of your mental, emotional, and physical energy. While these may not be single words like you used to describe your KVIs, describing specific observable red flag behaviors will make them easier to identify.

Building Your KVIs Into Your Day

Cultivating vitality is intentional and requires deliberate actions, and by doing so, you create a sense of personal agency and ownership. Throughout your day, you can ask yourself: on a scale of one to five (with one: you are running on fumes, and five: you are firing on all cylinders), how are my KVIs trending?

Begin by checking in with yourself before the start of your workday, once throughout the day, and when you are shifting from work to home. Experiment to discover a pattern that works for you. Some people find it hard to assess their energy at first. This is usually because they are used to evaluating from their head—how they think about energy, thoughts, and feelings. Many of us have built psychological awareness to better understand our strengths and weaknesses, our triggers and mindsets, but have dedicated far less time to building our physiological awareness. But the body provides loads of important and useful information. When you are energy tracking, pay close attention to the physical sensations. The more mindfully you can connect what's happening in your head to what's happening in your body, the better you'll be at giving yourself what you really need to help you boost your Work Vitality Quotient to work in your stand-out zone. The point of regularly monitoring is not to wait until you are running on fumes to act.

One more clarification: this isn't a test you pass or fail. The purpose of monitoring your energy in relation to your KVIs isn't to be constantly full of energy or beat yourself up when things are off. Vitality is dynamic and so is the energy that feeds it; after all, it is generated by using and refueling it. Engaging in life and doing both hard things and enjoyable things uses energy! Ending a full day tired is normal. Ending it depleted is a different story.

PART
TWO

Dear Success,

is it time to rethink how
to achieve you?

4

The Success Traps

KEISHA'S organization had pegged her for its soon-to-be-vacant CFO role. During an executive retreat, she'd received the results of a 360-degree leadership assessment. The feedback was stellar in all categories. As I congratulated her on the results, she surprised me by confiding that she was contemplating taking herself out of the running for the position. She felt it would be impossible to give any more of herself to her work, let alone sustain the level of involvement she believed contributed to her results. Her summary was simple: "I love the company and people I work with, but an executive role isn't the time to step back and be less committed. That isn't fair to anyone. If I can't be all-in, I need to step out of the running for the CFO role. Besides, I just feel tired of facing the uphill battle. I'm not sure I have it in me to succeed."

Keisha was notoriously hardworking and focused. She was generous with her time and energy, and it was obvious that she didn't shy away from challenges. While these qualities had served her well, she believed the only way to maintain her performance and get everything done at the level she wanted required her to be all-in, all day, every day. Unfortunately, this approach was also chipping away at Keisha's confidence, causing her to confuse feeling tired with being incapable.

This conversation took place on the third day of an intimate retreat. Keisha wasn't a negative person, nor was she incapable of succeeding in the CFO role. I had observed firsthand her ability to balance optimism with realism when discussing the stress level that came with her job. But she also described how the years of sacrifice had impacted her health and relationships. Not only that, but the all-consuming nature of her role meant she felt pressured to put off travel and other interests that she longed to pursue. Her all-or-nothing approach plus her achievement orientation—and working within an intensely competitive environment where overwork was lauded—left Keisha feeling trapped.

This isn't a story unique to Keisha. I have found that many high-performing, passionate, driven people take on such beliefs about what is required to be successful. Her story highlights a common experience that many of us can relate to. When you are celebrated and recognized for your commitment and even promoted for this all-in approach, over time the edges between you and your work blur. It becomes harder to recognize how tightly your identity is intertwined with your achievements. As a result, you don't just see yourself as someone who works hard and is loyal; you are the person everyone counts on to go the extra mile. You get things done, solving the complex problems that others shy away from addressing. You stay late, come in early, answer every email, and save the day—regardless of the sacrifices needed. You don't book holidays months in advance: what if work is busy and people need you? Before you know it, work is the caveat to all personal plans, and life ends up being what you fit around it.

If this describes you, chances are that even when that identity and approach to success stops serving you and instead starts exhausting you, rather than reset expectations, take a break, or establish boundaries, you double down, pushing yourself even

Success traps
you when work
is the caveat to all
personal plans
and life is what you
fit around it.

———————————

harder. This is often how people like Keisha, who were once invigorated by their work, end up burned out by it.

When You Use Your Own Emotions Against Yourself

Emotions are powerful drivers of behavior. As you've learned, negative emotions have a particularly formidable force, and as such, we are strongly motivated to take actions in response that help us avoid or counteract these feelings. Although experiencing a range of emotions is human and healthy, when it comes to your beliefs about success and how they either align with or detract from your Work Vitality Quotient, a triad of emotions tends to have an outsized influence: fear, obligation, and guilt, each of which is amplified by exhaustion. In concert, these emotions often leave you feeling helpless and resentful and often initiate unfounded feelings of shame.

Experiencing fear, obligation, and guilt is not bad or wrong. In fact, as you'll discover more thoroughly in the next section, all emotions provide important information you can use to understand yourself, others, and your environment. However, this particular triad of emotions becomes damaging when you weaponize it to coerce yourself into decisions and behaviors that counter your best interests.

Case in point, a 2022 study published in the *Journal of Organizational Behavior* reported that even when people feel sick enough to take the day off, they feel guilty about resting or not recuperating quickly enough. So instead of focusing on getting better, they push themselves back to work even if it prolongs their experience of feeling sick.

An easy way to identify if the triad is negatively influencing your perspective and decisions is to look out for what I call "justification triggers." Justification triggers are what we use when overriding our better judgment and justifying our actions to ourselves or others. The justification trigger for fear often sounds like, "I *need* to—

I need to prepare this weekend; the presentation is a make-or-break situation." For obligation, "I *have to*—I have to work late tonight; other people are counting on me." And guilt is the all-too-familiar, "I *should*—I should say yes to that request; it could be a good opportunity for market exposure."

Left unaddressed, this emotional triad limits your performance potential by luring you into thinking you're doing what it takes to be successful when really what you are doing is taking from yourself.

The Success Traps
. . . .

At the heart of our relationship with work are four well-intentioned but faulty approaches to achieving and maintaining our foothold on success. I call these "success traps" because they trap you into believing they are what make you successful. Before we explore these traps, some words of warning:

What makes the beliefs driving each success trap *so hard* to shift is they are often embedded within your identity and tend to tangle themselves up in your sense of self-worth.

What makes the success traps *so dangerous* is that they are centered on your values and strengths but are distorted by fear, obligation, and guilt.

What makes them *so seductive* is that they are rooted in beliefs that have served you in the past.

What makes them *so deceptive* is that they lead to practices that work in the short term but rarely create sustained and fulfilling success. Instead, they keep you entrenched in your survival zone and, at worst, put you on the fast track to burnout.

We'll explore each individually in the coming chapters, but the basis of each success trap is rooted in the following beliefs:

1　Loving your work makes you burnout proof.

2　Always being available to help demonstrates your dedication.

3 Your work ethic demonstrated by long hours is your competitive advantage.

4 Holding yourself to the highest possible standards fuels your best work.

As we delve into these success traps, it's important to remember a few things. First, that vitality is personal and is not fostered by trying to be less of who you are or more of something you aren't. It's entirely okay for work to be a meaningful part of your life and identity. There is nothing wrong with loving your work, helping others, being driven, and striving for excellence—the values at the core of each success trap. In fact, working in alignment with your values, such as each just stated, is energizing and vitality boosting. However, it bears repeating that being motivated by what is in your best interest in the healthiest way is the key. So instead of trying to dim down what motivates you, we'll explore ways to address the beliefs and behaviors trapping you and shift them to better serve yourself, your values, and the success you desire.

The second important consideration as we dissect each trap is to remember that there is zero dispute that people have too much to do. There are some very toxic work cultures and some bad managers out there. Difficult relationships are emotionally exhausting. Feeling overlooked, not feeling psychologically safe, and being micromanaged are real stressors. An unfair environment that pushes people to work against their values and make moral compromises contributes more to burnout than hours worked. The success traps don't negate any of this. They are, however, centered on the internal pressure and expectations you put on yourself, pushing you out of the stand-out zone or sinking you deeper into the survival zone.

Lastly, we can't ignore how the first few years of the 2020s reshaped our relationship to work. Many people realized that having a perfect résumé, envy-worthy job title, and material success was unfulfilling. Much like Keisha, others realized the mental, emotional, physical, and spiritual toll their job was having across each facet of their life. While the answer may be to move on to a new workplace, if you simply repeat the same patterns and create the same success traps in a new workplace, the old problems will soon reappear.

When you can distinguish a workplace issue from a *work belief* issue, you can better identify the questions you need to ask, avoid repeating familiar patterns, and assess if what you're doing serves the goal of boosting your Work Vitality Quotient. So, let's take a closer look at each.

5

The Trap of Believing You're Burnout Proof

GREEN smoothies, or more specifically, spinach smoothies, became my obsession for a while. Packed with nutrients and claims of helping with cognitive clarity, these smoothies seemed the perfect way to up my veggie intake. So after Googling some recipes, I blended away. Placebo effect or not, I felt energized and clearheaded, so much so that I thought, why not try to maximize the health benefits? I began adding more spinach to each smoothie, eventually making it so dense that my husband started referring to it as my "spinach sludge."

For weeks, I happily sipped my sludge. That is, until one morning while out for a walk with my neighbor I felt a stitch in my left side. Assuming it was brought on by the vigorous walking too soon after eating, I thought nothing of it. But that pain didn't go away. By the afternoon the stabbing ache was so intense I landed in the emergency room with what turned out to be kidney stones. When my doctor asked if my diet had changed, I shared that the only real difference was the daily spinach smoothies. At this, he explained that oxalates from the spinach likely caused my kidney stones. I was consuming too much. Even with healthy leafy greens, it turns out that too much of a good thing can harm you.

This story represents what I call the "spinach principle." It describes what happens when we take something good and overdo it, canceling its benefits. The same applies to work and our beliefs about burnout. Being committed, involved, and passionate can serve as strengths that have healthy, enhancing, and protective benefits from burnout. But when overused and overdone, the benefits become obsolete. The spinach principle lays the foundation for the first success trap: the belief that loving your work makes you burnout proof.

When Committed Becomes Consumed

Initially, you invest in your work because you are committed to what you do, excited about the opportunities, and motivated by the joy you get from doing it. And then over time, the dedication gives way to desire, and you start to invest more, working harder to get ahead. Maybe that's to close more deals, launch more products, build a bigger team, expand to new locations, or gain new followers. Soon you find yourself needing to work even harder just to keep up, which requires more and more of your time and energy— DMs all day, double-booked appointments, emails in bed, or conference calls during vacation. And suddenly, all you seem to do is work!

People caution that you're too attached and overly invested, that prioritizing work above all else will burn you out. You resist, believing your circumstances are different because your job is meaningful and important, you care so much, or you love what you do. And still, deep down, you feel like all the pressure is on your shoulders and worry things will fall apart if you don't keep stepping up. All the while, you know the joy you started with is harder to find. The excitement has turned into exhaustion. And where you once felt committed to your work, you now feel completely consumed by it.

Again and again, I see people so overinvested in their work that a simple setback gets interpreted as a failure. Feedback, even when developmental in nature, is received as a personal attack. Any suggestion of alternative approaches, perspectives, or ideas are fought, criticized, or dismissed. All negative repercussions get explained away and defended by the fact that you are so passionate, your goals are so meaningful, and the results are so significant that everything else is secondary. Not only does this approach plateau promising careers, but it also directly siphons off any potentially positive effects being invested in your work could provide. Here are some telltale signs that your work commitment has turned into consuming overinvestment:

- You pour so much of yourself into your job that you don't have anything left for other areas of your life.

- Work tends to control your emotions; if it goes well you're having a good day, if it goes badly, the day is a write-off.

- Work is a zero-sum game. One day you claim, "I'm done! I've given everything to this job and for what?!" The next day you're working from your hotel room as your family goes to the beach, even after you promised you wouldn't work on your vacation.

- The energy you invest into work is consistently greater than the energy you get out.

- You feel taken for granted and resentful but continue sacrificing your needs in the name of work.

The Passion Tax

Complicating matters is that overinvestment in your work is often mislabeled as "passion." Researchers from Duke University's

Being consumed
by your work
is not the same as
being committed
to your work.

Fuqua School of Business found that when employees were perceived as being passionate, it was considered more acceptable—
and in some cases expected—for them to work on weekends,
do extra unpaid work, and handle tasks not in their job description.
The thinking is, if you love what you do, why wouldn't you just
do more of it? Passion exploitation sounds like this: "Get Mel to do
it. She won't mind; she loves this stuff and would probably do it
anyway."

At a previous job, I was doing a lot of travel, which I loved, but
I was finding the travel logistics on top of all my other responsibilities overwhelming. I had been promised additional resources
that had not come through yet. The tipping point came when I
mistakenly flew into Washington, DC, when in fact my work was in
Washington State. Luckily, I had time to book a new flight and get
to the right location, but with a significant contract on the line, it
was stressful to say the least. I spoke to my boss about it, and their
response was, "I thought you loved traveling?" Too much of something, even when you love it, can still be too much.

When unfair environments grounded in harmful and exploit-
ative attitudes make you feel as if you are constantly needing to
prove yourself while simultaneously feeling taken advantage of,
your susceptibility to burnout is heightened. To be clear, this is not
a "you problem": it is a workplace culture problem. While having
conversations to address your concerns is a critical step, separating
who you are from what you do is where you do have control.

Going from Consumed Back to Committed

If this is a trap you've found yourself in, you've probably had friends
and loved ones tell you that you need to stop giving so much to
your work. But the challenge is that not contributing your best or
not caring doesn't align with your values. Doing work that is meaningful to you does. Add to this that trying to be less of you rarely

boosts vitality. So, how do you extract yourself from the enticing snare of overinvestment while staying aligned with your values and not being taken advantage of?

You start by acknowledging that being committed to your work is not the same as being consumed by it. To make this adjustment in your thinking, apply a simple reframe. Instead of trying to make yourself care less about your work, reframe it to reclaiming your vitality at work.

You then need to accept that the only thing you can control is yourself—your approach to work, how you respond to requests, and most importantly, how much energy you invest in your work relative to the rest of your life. This will allow you to separate your sense of fulfillment, success, and self-worth from the validation of others.

Getting out of the emotional weeds requires eschewing your amygdala-driven, all-or-nothing thinking and tapping into your pre-frontal cortex's wonder circuitry. A powerful question to get you out of feeling like you need to prove your value and into a stand-out zone frame of mind is to ask yourself: what decisions would I make, what actions would I take, and what perspectives would I hold if I felt twice as strong, valued, and confident?

From this vantage point, you may see that no matter how much sweat, time, and loyalty you invest into your work, it is still only your job. While you might be doing life-changing work, your job is not your whole life. Your workplace is not the center of the universe. Nor is it the only place to work or the only job you can do. And finally, that you have the agency and options to plug the leaks of overinvested energy and redirect that energy to other areas, including people and activities that will make you feel empowered and alive instead. Each of which is in your control.

If you need a reason bigger than honoring yourself to withdraw your overinvestment in work—especially if that workplace takes you for granted—consider the people in your life who care about you. They are investing in you so you can do what you love. But instead of getting the return on investment they deserve, they watch as you use that investment to give to people and places that don't value it. As difficult as it is to see in the moment, not choosing to change how and where you give your time, energy, and attention is still a choice.

As early as 492 BC, Confucius offered advice that can be translated today as, "Choose a job you love, and you'll never work a day in your life." Loving your work will undoubtedly boost your Work Vitality Quotient. But let's be clear, what Confucius did not say was, "Choose a job you love, and you'll never need anything else in your life." Doing work that you love, that you are committed to, that feels meaningful and fulfilling, is undeniably vitality boosting, *provided* you are working in a healthy way. When you become so consumed by your work that it controls your feelings, behaviors, and self-image, it not only becomes unhealthy but also makes you more prone to burnout versus protecting you from it.

Instead of believing that loving your work makes you burnout proof, the updated work relationship belief that strengthens your Work Vitality Quotient is that no one is burnout proof, but loving your work *and* having a full life are powerful buffers *against* burnout.

6

The Trap of Always Being Available

I'M RARELY late, especially when it comes to travel. I like arriving early and having time to relax. And yet, despite my best efforts, sometimes the universe has a different plan for me.

One notable example of this occurred at my hometown airport. I had arrived at my usual early time and was met by a check-in line that extended all the way down the terminal. As someone who travels often between Canada and the United States, I have a global entry pass that provides expedited security and customs clearance. It typically takes me around fifteen minutes to get through, half an hour on a slow day.

As I walked through the airport and past the long line of people, I thought to myself, "Good thing I'm early and have global entry because there are definitely people in that line who are going to miss their flight." But as I neared the security area, it became clear that the long line of people I had just walked by were also waiting for global entry, which meant I had to do the embarrassing turnaround and walk back past all those same people to take my spot at the end of the line.

After well over two hours of waiting, I was a few people back from clearing security when I overheard a conversation. A security officer stationed at the luggage scanning machine approached the agent scanning boarding passes and said, "I need to go on my break." Hoping my facial expression went unnoticed, I immediately thought to myself, "Come on, look how busy it is! Take your break once things settle down. People need to catch their flights." Based on the eye rolling and audible sighs of others in line, I knew I wasn't the only one thinking this.

The agent scanning the boarding passes exasperatedly said, "Can't you just stay out? We're so backed up." To which the security officer replied, "I came in early to cover the short staffing and have already worked through my first break—I need to take a break."

"Well, if it's more important than just helping us clear this line, that's your call," the boarding pass agent replied, while all of us travelers attempted to sway the luggage scanner with our eyes to keep working so we could make our flights. Visibly frustrated, he shook his head and continued working.

The boarding pass agent gave him a big smile and said, "Thanks for being so helpful."

The Hidden Beliefs behind Being Helpful

Have you ever been celebrated for overriding a boundary to accommodate a request, even when saying yes came at a cost to you? The answer, most certainly, is yes. What about the other way? Have you ever been punished directly or indirectly for holding a boundary and saying no to someone's request? The answer is likely also yes. Or perhaps you found that last question confusing because you've never considered saying no.

The reactions of those standing in line at the airport reflected a pair of often subconscious but widely held beliefs:

- Putting the needs of our work or others above ourselves is a sign of dedication.

- If we are available, we should help, because that is what good people do.

This energy-zapping combo forms the second success trap—believing that always being available to help is a demonstration of your dedication. But there are a couple of flawed assumptions here. First is mistakenly believing that giving all of ourselves all of the time is a representation of dedication. The second is not as evident: mistakenly believing that being reachable is the same as being available to help. Yes, we may be technically reachable by our devices—our colleagues know that if we're out, we likely have our phones with us. However, just because we can be reached doesn't mean we're available (mentally, emotionally, or physically) to stop what we're doing and help, nor should it.

The Curse of Constant Reachability

We've all done it. You're happily catching up with a good friend you haven't seen in a while, and just as they are in the middle of sharing an important update on life, your phone vibrates in your pocket. Without even hesitating, you take out your phone and look down to see who just texted. When you look back up at your friend, the conversation awkwardly trails off…

Now consider a different scenario. If that texter barged in on your conversation in person and started talking over your other friend, you'd probably angrily interject to point out that they'd just interrupted a meaningful conversation. But when that same person texts, regardless of what you are doing, you feel a need to interrupt the *in-person* conversation you're engaged in to find out who it is.

In our digitally connected world, where our phones come with us everywhere we go, anyone is a simple text, email, or DM away.

We are now reachable almost anywhere and anytime, including when we're sleeping, on vacation, eating dinner, or in a conversation with a good friend at a party. The borders between professional time and personal time are increasingly difficult to distinguish. The consequence of being so reachable is that it quickly translates into feeling obligated to always be immediately available to address ever-mounting workloads, to take meetings at any hour, or to be continuously responsive.

The Lack of Work-Life Boundaries

Not long after many people started working from home during the initial wave of the COVID-19 pandemic, I overheard a conversation between a couple while standing in line for a takeout order. One said to the other, "Did I tell you? With the remote policies, they are giving us work phones. Now we'll need to be available all of the time." It's not that this person believed they should be checking email at all hours; they believed they had to. That is the problem with confusing being reachable for being available to respond.

While work-life balance is a concept everyone is familiar with, it is also one few people believe is achievable. A potentially more realistic concept revolves around establishing work-life boundaries. Since you are essentially always reachable, think of work-life boundaries as setting parameters of when you are available to respond to work requests and when you are not. These boundaries are independent of how reachable you technically are or what activities you are engaged in (if anything). In truth, many people, like the ones I unintentionally eavesdropped on standing in line, have never considered having a conversation with their boss, colleagues, employees, or clients about after-work expectations and availability, let alone personally setting and holding themselves accountable to boundaries.

Availability creep always results in resentment.

Watch the Availability Creep
. . . .

Further complicating the reachable/available dynamic is a phenomenon I call "availability creep." Recognizing and intercepting it will
only become more critical with increasing remote, hybrid, and flex
working arrangements. The premise is that the more responsive
you have been in the past, the more available people will expect
you to be in the future. When you neglect to set or communicate
or actively override your boundaries, initially, people interpret this
as you going the extra mile for them. But do this a few times, and
people will normalize this behavior. Suddenly what was once you
"going the extra mile" is now just the status quo expectation—and
asking for a little more from you next time doesn't seem like a big
deal, which as you now know, is even more prevalent if you are perceived as being passionate and dedicated to your work.

If you regularly answer emails on the weekend, why wouldn't
people expect you to do the same on your holidays? And since
you're already online and checking email while away on vacation,
couldn't you just jump on a conference call? And when you communicate boundaries by, for example, setting an out-of-office email
reply but then continue to answer email, your actions show people
that they should ignore your words.

This progressive boundary pushing creates a negatively reinforcing relationship between your sense of obligation to accommodate
and other people's ever-growing levels of expectation. Eventually,
the rising expectations become impossible to meet. The end result
is almost always resentment.

So, how do you shift the belief that being constantly available to
help is a demonstration of your dedication?

What Do You Gain? What Do You Lose?
. . . .

It starts by tapping into your wonder circuitry with a set of agency-
creating questions. Even when a behavior seems illogical, we need

to remember that due to the brain's natural instincts, people *are motivated to do things because there is something in it for them; either to gain something or avoid losing something.* This is another reason why we often don't do the things we know we should.

Psychologists label these instinctual responses as promotion- or prevention-focused change motivation. Promotion-focused change motivation describes the tendency to be motivated toward positive rewards and taking actions that promote beneficial outcomes. Prevention-focused change motivation describes the tendency to be motivated away from negative consequences, taking preventive measures to avoid bad outcomes.

In my coaching practice, I find some of the most powerful insights come from bringing awareness to why people are doing something that goes against what they say they want. Specifically, what people gain by proceeding with a behavior (promotion based) and what they potentially lose that is most important to them (prevention based). Relating these questions to boundaries, you might ask yourself:

1   What do I gain by not working with boundaries (or staying the same as I am now)?

Common answers include: Being liked, making others happy by putting their needs first, demonstrating love, building a positive reputation, competitive advantages, financial rewards, faster career progression, an ego boost, feeling in control, being helpful, feeling valuable and needed, avoiding conflict, job security.

2   What do I lose by not working with boundaries (or staying the same as I am now)?

Common answers include: Healthy relationships, time with friends and family, time for fun and hobbies and meaningful life goals, happiness, peace of mind, personal health, well-being, the respect of others, feeling aligned with values, confidence, trust, being a role model, integrity, being dependable, performance, success, developing others, job progression.

Chances are that your answers to each question strongly align with what matters most to you. With these desires in mind, ask yourself the following:

3 What is a healthier way I can achieve the gains (and simultaneously address the losses) while still working with boundaries?

We often assume that if people lack boundaries, it is because they are people-pleasers. But reflecting on the questions above reveals that this single assumption is an oversimplification. Many people work without boundaries or abandon them if they fear it will negatively impact their relationships, reputation, or safety. However, other very valid factors need to be considered as the rewards of working with loose or no boundaries at all—real or perceived— as these, too, are strong motivators. Still, stay alert to your brain's attempt to convince you with all-or-nothing thinking that you can *only* achieve these gains by working without boundaries, as it is seldom true. This is what makes the third question so important. Many of the gains we *believe* we get from not having boundaries *can* be achieved—more sustainably and without the losses—by actually having boundaries if we are intentional in our approach. Working with boundaries is not a trade-off; it's a win-win.

As importantly, your brain is strongly loss averse. Composing a robust list of potential losses that deeply align with your values will help build the motivation and courage to put changes in place. Reflecting on these questions often reveals that many of the same perceived gains you get by working without boundaries can or will eventually become losses. No one can be available 24/7 or accommodate every request and maintain the quality of their work, let alone preserve the creativity, focus, and enthusiasm that allows them to work and live from their stand-out zone.

Rethinking Boundaries
. . . .

I want to be very clear: making yourself available to help others is not a problem. So what is?

Doing it because you have self-weaponized a sense of obligation to your work and others without protecting yourself—is.

Doing it because you believe being helpful requires being selfless—is.

Doing it without boundaries that clarify what your help consists of or when and how you can best offer it—is.

Establishing, communicating, and holding boundaries can be a scary and tricky shift when it feels like—or you actually are—going against what you, others, or your workplace values. For example, on the one hand, many organizations and society at large praise people who are willing to override their boundaries in the name of being a good team player and then celebrate them for their tireless work. On the other hand, rarely are people applauded for their stellar boundaries.

On an individual basis, if you are someone who deeply values being of service and thus willingly gives your time, energy, and expertise to help, the idea of saying no to an incoming request can conflict with your self-image. Complicating matters is that often, without even realizing it, we use our level of mental, emotional, and physical exhaustion as a measure of our helpfulness. The more exhausted you are, the more dedicated you must be! The challenge is that each of these examples provides the very same reason why you end up in meetings you shouldn't be in, take on additional work when someone leaves without renegotiating expectations and priorities, say yes to projects that are outside your wheelhouse of interest or expertise, or deplete yourself by endlessly giving to others who never give anything back.

In truth, always being available and helping people regardless of the cost isn't proving your dedication; it's undermining your potential. Instead, remember that your boundaries can be flexible, so you

Establishing
and honoring
boundaries
are signs of
your dedication
to be helpful.

have the liberty to adjust or change them when needed, but now you can challenge your assumptions and make decisions with full awareness of what is motivating you.

There will always be people who need you. Rarely will your to-do list be clear. There will undoubtedly continue to be conflicting priorities. And, no one is going to set, or hold, your boundaries for you. Instead of thinking of boundaries as restrictions, view them as enablers. Every thoughtful, compassionately communicated, boundary-driven "no" frees you to say yes to the people, projects, and pursuits that matter the most. Boundary by boundary is how you create the space—mentally, emotionally, and physically—to increase your Work Vitality Quotient.

An Inconvenient Truth

Before we close off this success trap, let's go back to the moment I judged the security officer for requesting his break. Later that evening, I reflected on the interaction, only to be met with an uncomfortable realization. Had there not been a line and had I not been running late, I'm fairly certain my perspective would have been different. My loyalties would have been with the agent who requested a break. I suspect I would have thought, "That security officer has every right to a break, and good on him for taking care of himself instead of just focusing on work and the needs of others." If I felt extra judgmental, I probably would have thought, "This is what's wrong with our society today. We expect people to put work over everything else—it's no wonder people are so burned out!"

So, now for the part that might sting (it certainly did for me). Most people agree that there needs to be better harmony between our personal and professional worlds and fully support their colleagues, employees, and customers to set clear boundaries to achieve it. That is, *until it inconveniences us*. We support people to say no more—unless it benefits us for them to say yes. In truth, talking about values is easy. Living by those values is easy when it's convenient. Living those values when it's inconvenient is when it counts *and* is when it is most challenging.

"Always-on" cultures are made up of "always-on" people. If we want to create vitality-driven organizations, then we must realize that each of us either contributes to the problem we complain about or the solution we are longing for. You contribute to the solution when you communicate and work within your availability boundaries, but as importantly, when you recognize that just because someone is reachable, doesn't mean they are available to respond. Be gracious in respecting the boundaries of others—especially when it's inconvenient.

Instead of believing that always being available to help is a demonstration of your dedication, the updated work relationship belief that strengthens your Work Vitality Quotient is that establishing and honoring boundaries are signs of your dedication to truly be helpful.

7

The Trap of Equating More Hours with Advantage

ETHAN was a hardworking young lawyer employed at an extremely competitive firm. He had big goals and, according to his colleagues, was crushing them. He put in long hours building a large book of business, making the possibility of becoming an equity partner a reality much sooner than he'd planned. But while working on a potentially promotion-solidifying case, things started to turn. After getting twelve hours of sleep over the course of four days, he submitted a brief in which opposing counsel found a critical citation error with trial-impacting consequence. If that was not bad enough, he was to present at a partners' meeting the following morning but slept through it. In a matter of days, his impeccable reputation was unraveling.

Prisha was a part-time elementary school teacher who recently learned she was in the running to be hired full-time for the following school year. She also had a lucrative side business in direct sales, with an extensive sales network. She was enthusiastic, had high energy, and loved nothing more than getting things done and conquering goals. Being busy was her brand, and she wore it proudly. Between growing her sales business and taking courses to strengthen her teaching résumé, she always had a lot on the go and often worked late into the night.

Feeling worn out from the week of teaching and following a frustrating interaction with a customer late on a Friday evening, she hammered out a text to a friend. Contrary to Prisha's usual tone and nature, her text was mocking and disparaging and threw the legitimacy of her product and the direct sales company under the bus. This wouldn't have been a problem, really, except she accidentally sent the text to the customer instead of her friend. Within hours the text was posted on social media, and within days had spread throughout her online and professional communities. By Monday morning, not only had she lost a significant number of customers, but parents were calling the school where she worked, questioning the appropriateness of her being a teacher.

Two different people, two different situations, one common success trap. Both attributed their success to their ability and drive to put in long, hard hours. While their work ethic undoubtedly contributed to their success, the challenge is that neither was able to recognize the tipping point when more hours worked *stopped being an asset* and instead *became a liability*. Not only that, but both told me that friends, colleagues, and loved ones had warned them that the pace they were going at was unsustainable. Yet they both still believed that going heads down and pushing through would result in better outcomes—an approach which ultimately led to their downfalls. We've all heard stories of hardworking people physically and psychologically crashing just short of the finish line of their most important goals. When, as with Ethan and Prisha, this happens because of a misguided belief about what it takes to be successful, it is that much more unfortunate.

The Myth of More Hours

Underlying Ethan's and Prisha's actions is a deep-seated belief that many of us hold: more work results in better outcomes. We convince ourselves we'll get double the output if we put in a sixteen-hour day over an eight-hour day. While this can be true in very short spurts, there is always a point of diminishing returns. Not to mention, it has even become an insinuation of laziness or an insult of doing the bare minimum if someone *only* works "normal office hours" *even when they are getting their work done.* A couple of years ago, as I was starting my company, a well-meaning friend gifted me a coffee cup with the inscription: *Secret to Success: Hustle 24/7 while everyone else just works their 9–5.* The message that more hours worked (especially compared to others) equates to bigger, faster, and more visible success seems to be reinforced everywhere, including in my cupboard!

Even if you're feeling more overstretched and overcommitted by the minute, I'll wager that you've probably also said things like, "I feel bad; I was so unproductive today!" We feel too busy to rest and then feel guilty if we do.

Productivity Isn't the Villain

The goal of productivity is to be more efficient so you can get more done in a shorter amount of time. Ideally being productive *frees up* time for you to engage in other areas of life, including using that time to rest and refuel. But it seems we've missed the point. We've transformed the goal of productivity into getting more done in less time—just so we can get even more done—filling up all of our time. It's like living in a perpetual hotdog-eating contest where the reward for scarfing down the most hotdogs is more hotdogs.

It is this should-always-do-more thinking that trapped both Ethan and Prisha to keep taking on more, pushing themselves to their limits with long hours, stopping only when it was too late. If you find yourself lured into the trap of believing that long hours and outworking others is your competitive advantage, then it is important to first acknowledge that *productive work* is not the same as *overwork*. For both Ethan and Prisha this distinction became blurred. What complicated matters was that they enjoyed their work and often the long hours worked were a choice, not an expectation, which is why they neglected to heed the warnings offered by others.

First off, for those with a strong sense of drive, you know that it's often the hard, productive, meaningful work that makes you feel most alive. Long hours working alongside trusted colleagues can be exhilarating when a promising opportunity gets your adrenaline pumping and the possibilities are palpable. And when you're doing work that lights you up, that puts you in a state of flow, long days fly by. You can—and do—tend to work more when you have control over your work, are supported in it, and feel positively challenged by it. There is nothing wrong with any of this. The problem occurs when you convince yourself that the damaging consequences of overwork don't apply to you. The fact is that long hours are rarely sustainable without adequate recovery. Even the most passionate, ambitious, committed brains need rest. The point isn't to say how many hours are too many, the point is to recognize the difference between working in your stand-out zone versus the survival zone.

Being Busy Isn't the Same as Being Productive

Unfortunately, when it comes to overwork, we often confuse being busy with being productive. Just because we're doing a lot, doesn't mean we're doing it well. Harvard professor and researcher Dr. Teresa Amabile finds that when we feel pressured to get more work done, either because of external pressures such as a deadline or internal pressures such as guilt, we do get more done—for a time—but the trade-off is that we accomplish less *great work*.

Working in your
stand-out zone requires
recognizing when
putting in more hours
stops being an asset and
starts becoming
a liability.

One of the reasons this happens is that when we're too busy and become overstretched, our brain's natural desire for comfort and reward means we have a not-so-helpful tendency to focus on the low-hanging fruit. As a result, we conflate important, meaningful work with easy, urgent, and often mundane tasks. Additionally, we tend to *overfocus on task lists* and *under-focus on relationships*. As a result, we act less collaboratively and engage less empathetically. Combined, these factors lead to more ineffective meetings being booked, more angry emails sent, and more time needed to clean up mistakes and clear up misunderstandings. But perhaps the least recognized reason less great work is being accomplished is because we get caught in a cycle of effectively stealing creativity, energy, and effectiveness from tomorrow to meet today's demands.

Productivity Hangovers

I'm sure you've had days like this: You blazed through a to-do list, crossing items off and even accomplishing some tasks that weren't on the list, which, of course, you added to the list just so you could feel the satisfaction of crossing them off. While the day was long, you went to bed thinking, "Now I have time to do the important stuff tomorrow!" only to wake up feeling groggy, unmotivated, and easily distracted. If this sounds familiar, you have experienced a productivity hangover. Just as an alcohol-induced hangover results from too much drinking, a productivity hangover is a result of too much *doing*.

Productivity hangovers are neurological in nature. While crossing items off your to-do list can give you an energy rush that propels you through the day, the prefrontal cortex has limited bandwidth and fatigues with long hours, especially when you're drawing on cognitively expensive resources. This, after all, is one reason you sleep: to give your body and brain time to clean up and restock the supplies that have been used up or are running low. Even doing simple things you enjoy will eventually tire the prefrontal cortex, which, as you know, is responsible for creativity, complex thinking, and values-based decision making. The longer you push the prefrontal cortex to perform, the more time and quality recovery practices are needed to restore the depleted resources.

Predicting Future Feelings

Our susceptibility to productivity hangovers arises because, according to Daniel Gilbert, a Harvard psychology professor, we have a hard time predicting how we'll feel in the future. Not only do we overestimate what will make us happy—"Once I get this stuff done, then I'll feel I've done enough!"—but we also tend to believe that how we feel in the moment is how we'll feel in the future. Meaning that when we're tired, we discount strategies such as taking an exercise break, believing nothing will change how tired we feel. But equally, if we feel energized to get things done today, we assume that the same energy will be available tomorrow. As such, we again dismiss any suggestion of a break to protect and replenish that drawn-upon energy and keep pushing on. Energy—whether physical, mental, or emotional—is finite and must be replenished to be sustained. Without adequate time for rest and recovery, the energy we are counting on may not be there tomorrow.

Estimating Time Needed

There is also an interesting dynamic between our activities and time which contributes to overwork-driven productivity hangovers. Once, while trying to coordinate access to the bathroom with my graduate school roommate, I asked how long it took her to get ready in the morning. "It depends on how much time I have," she said. "If I have fifteen minutes, then it takes me fifteen minutes. If I have an hour, it takes an hour." Her answer didn't help us coordinate our schedules, but it did stay with me. The same idea applies to work. A task will expand to fill the time allotted for its completion. It is called Parkinson's Law; a cautionary tale meant to motivate us to manage our time better. But it also explains why the more time we give to work, the more work fills that time. Parkinson's Law is worsened by the fact that not only are we bad at predicting how we'll feel in the future, but we are also notoriously bad at predicting how much time something will require. Known as the planning fallacy, we tend to underestimate how long something will take to do and overestimate how much we can get done within a slated amount of time. If you have ever made a to-do list thirty items long and then come to the end of the day and only have four things crossed off your list, then you know this is true. Unsurprisingly, our prediction accuracy only worsens the more tired we get, which consequently results in the need to work longer hours to address our overcommitments, making us even more susceptible to productivity hangovers.

So what is the antidote to this negatively reinforcing cycle? Of each success trap, this is perhaps the one most influenced by workplace cultures. As such, it is imperative to recognize that at a societal level, we have normalized overwork and morphed it into an admirable work ethic. While changing this on the grand scale is no easy feat, recognizing how our work ethic identity is driving our actions and shifting it when it keeps us locked in the survival zone is a promising start. This begins by personally ceasing to define our work ethic by what we're willing to sacrifice and redefining it to incorporate our commitment to taking the needed actions that ensure we can make our highest and healthiest contribution from the stand-out zone. Two things within your control will help you to make this shift.

Workdays Should Start and End

Especially in the world of hybrid work, where your office is usually mere steps away from your kitchen table, living room sofa, and even your bed, the data clearly demonstrates the benefits of establishing core "work" hours. Perhaps even more specifically, establishing when your workday begins and when it ends. These can be a linear set of hours from morning to evening (perhaps aligning with your organization's core hours), or if you have the flexibility, you might work in segments.

Establishing a standardized start and end time for my workday has been both the hardest and most beneficial change I've made over the last five years. Because of my personal experience, my clients' experiences, as well as the unquestionable research backing it up, it is also the first strategy I suggest implementing for those who are tired of feeling like all they do is work, eat, sleep, and repeat. Among the many benefits I've noticed, one of significant importance is that I'm more mindful of how much I can realistically accomplish in a day. Proving the validity of Parkinson's Law that work will expand to fill the time you give it, I work more productively during my core work hours because I know there is a limited amount of time to get things done. Having a predetermined end to my workday removes the option to push things off to the evening, which is what I used to do when I was too tired or overcommitted in the day to address everything. In truth, what often happened was something that should have taken fifteen minutes to complete with focus during the day ended up taking an hour and a half in the evening. This then cut into my time to rest and refuel, making me increasingly less effective the next day, further depleting my energy and prolonging the cycle. Recognizing this pattern's impact prompted me to designate it as one of my KVI survival zone red flags.

Will your working hours need to be flexible at times? Of course! However, the nuance of sticking to them is that the more consistently you do, the more energy you will have, creating a positively reinforcing cycle that keeps you in your stand-out zone. And while this is the goal, there's a rub: it is also where the seduction of the "more hours, more advantage" trap sets in. When feeling vital you start to convince yourself that if you have more energy in the tank and hours in the day, and you *could* get more done, then you should.

We have
normalized overwork
and morphed it
into an admirable
work ethic.

_____

This is precisely what I found. While the tactical strategy of pre-establishing an end of the workday time made sense logically, I would often override it if I felt it was violating my work ethic. Remember, vitality is as much about perspective as it is about practices.

Your Work Ethic Needs a Rest Ethic

Like Ethan and Prisha, many of us are driven by our work ethic. But to overcome this success trap, we must realize that having a strong work ethic is only half of the equation. It needs to be complimented with as solid of a rest ethic. While we will explore how your beliefs about rest influence your decisions in the last part of the book focused on re-energizing you, John Fitch and Max Frenzel, authors of *Time Off: A Practical Guide to Building Your Rest Ethic and Finding Success without the Stress*, provide a powerful analogy. They equate a work ethic to our inhale and a rest ethic to our exhale, sharing, "just as a deep exhale prepares you for a better inhale, your rest ethic enables you to have a better work ethic."

In the context of boosting your Work Vitality Quotient, your work ethic commits you to contribute your best work. In contrast, your rest ethic commits you to switch gears and engage in vitality-boosting practices that invest in tomorrow's effectiveness versus overworking which ultimately steals from it. In addition to rest and recovery, this includes living a full, healthy life outside of work. Just as you can't only inhale, you also can't expect a work ethic alone to be enough. After all, vitality is generated by both using it *and* refueling it.

Instead of believing that working more hours gives you an edge at work, the updated work relationship belief that strengthens your Work Vitality Quotient is that working from your stand-out zone (and as importantly, realizing when you are not) is your unique competitive advantage.

8

The Trap of the
Highest Standards

REMEMBER Keisha from chapter 4? "All-in, all day, every day" was the formula she believed led to her success. It was also why she was considering taking her name out of the running for the CFO position.

"What if it didn't need to be so hard?" I asked her in a one-on-one coaching session.

"What if you were to show yourself some of the same compassion you so generously give to others?" Confused, she looked at me as if I'd just suggested she grow wings and fly.

Like many hard-driving people I've studied, Keisha was trapped in the mistaken belief that holding herself to the highest standards fueled her best work. Now, I know what you are thinking—high standards, along with being ambitious, goal-focused, and self-disciplined are often characteristics attributed to successful people like Keisha. They are, and none of these makes for a success trap. But holding yourself to unattainably high standards in the process, well, that is another thing altogether.

Keisha is what I call a horizon-line chaser. Anytime she met a goal or got close to a standard, instead of acknowledging the achievement or celebrating the progress, she raised the expectations and set the goalpost further away. Her standards were on the horizon, impossible to ever meet. I suspect many people reading this would identify themselves as horizon-line chasers, even proudly so.

Keisha was a woman working in a male-dominated industry and from her perspective, being "as good" as others was never an option. She had to be better. While she admitted she could be a bit of a perfectionist and was quite tough on herself, she believed these characteristics pushed her to be her best. Anything less than holding herself to uncompromisingly high standards felt in direct conflict with her values. This is why she initially interpreted the suggestion of exercising more self-compassion as letting her guard down and taking it easy on herself, which in her words, "Frankly, feels irresponsible and self-indulgent."

Theodore Roosevelt is famously quoted as saying, "Nothing worthwhile comes easy." People who are driven by a strong personal desire to accomplish meaningful and important goals often unconsciously interpret this to mean: if it matters, it should be hard. Sadly, this translates into some damaging viewpoints, including:

- Successful people are super busy and exhausted.

- Superhuman effort is required 110 percent of the time.

- You can't just meet expectations—you must exceed them.

- It's not enough to just be good and perform; you must be better than you've ever been and overperform.

- Either you're perfect, or you're a failure.

This thinking is at the heart of the all-in, all day, every day mindset that Keisha, along with many other high achievers, holds.

Skeptical of Self-Compassion

While researching this book, I attended a self-compassion and meditation workshop. The facilitator opened the workshop by asking how many people knew they were too hard on themselves. Almost everyone in the room put up their hand. She then asked how many people believed that showing support and compassion to their friends and family was critical to the health of those relationships. Every hand shot up. "So, why do we have such a hard time being kind to ourselves?" she asked. There was a collective hesitation.

My guess is that few of you would disagree that demonstrating compassion to others is a positive quality. And yet, if this is a trap you find yourself getting snagged by, I suspect that if someone suggests you show that same level of compassion to yourself when a mistake is made or a goal is missed, you are met with an internal sense of resistance. Perhaps, as with Keisha, it is because of a widely held misconception that if you are kind to yourself, you will become complacent. Or that settling for anything less than perfection will result in subpar results. Both feed the belief that celebrating achievements might dampen your drive or cause you to take your eye off the prize. So instead, you relentlessly strive, pushing yourself forward by setting expectations far higher than anyone else would expect of you. Then you beat yourself up when you fall short of them or move the goalpost when you achieve them. It's little wonder you're so exhausted.

The Perfectionist Myth

While perfectionism can be detrimental, there is a reason why so many of us have responded with "I'm too much of a perfectionist" when asked about our weaknesses. We believe that perfectionists do better work, devote more hours, and are more engaged. But before you start scripting your perfectionist humblebrag for your next job interview, consider the flip side.

In a 2018 *Harvard Business Review* article, researchers shared the results of one of the most extensive studies ever conducted on the performance effects of perfectionism. To test whether perfectionists were better performers at work, they conducted a meta-analysis of ninety-five studies ranging from 1980 to 2018. The answer was simple. Performance and perfectionism were not positively or negatively related to one another. In other words, perfectionists were no better (or worse) at their job than non-perfectionists.

How can this be? It turns out that people with perfectionistic tendencies may do stellar work, devote more hours, and be more invested in the outcomes; however, they are also more likely to set rigid and excessively high standards and evaluate their behavior overly critically while at the same time dismissing positive feedback on their performance. As a result, the simplest answer as to why perfectionism doesn't result in better performance is that the extra hours, angst, and investment put in to get things perfect is rarely worth the other compromises needed to achieve it or the time and energy lost doing it. This then leads to higher levels of stress, anxiety, and burnout, each potentially negatively affecting performance factors such as creative and strategic thinking, emotional intelligence, resilience, and overall effectiveness. As such, perfectionistic tendencies tend to wash away any advantages they gain.

We drain our Work Vitality Quotient with unrealistic expectations in the form of perfectionism, which feeds on fear, breeds constant dissatisfaction, and elicits self-criticism. However, when high standards result in healthy striving, learning in the face of setbacks, and ownership of our contributions, then we strengthen our Work Vitality Quotient. The difference between toxic perfectionism and healthy striving involves taking a kind but realistic view of your experiences and expectations. This is the essence of self-compassion.

The benefits of self-compassion, research suggests, are that when people respond to difficulty with self-compassion, they more

Self-compassion
is about learning
how to have your
own back.

———————

willingly take responsibility for their behaviors, more accurately evaluate their performance and shortcomings, and are more likely to view those shortcomings as changeable and thus grow from them.

What's more, self-compassion matters neurologically as well. When you put yourself down as a means of pushing yourself forward, you trigger your fight-or-flight system. The amygdala is ill-equipped to differentiate between a real threat and a perceived one. When you tell yourself you suck and allow that critical inner voice to pick away at your performance and thus confidence, your amygdala believes you. So even when your self-evaluations are needlessly and unrealistically harsh, you flood your system with unnecessary cortisol, making it more difficult to access your prefrontal cortex and diminishing your abilities to bring your best forward.

Add to this, you train yourself to feel unfulfilled by positive experiences when you fail to give them the consideration they deserve. Time and attention are how your hippocampus learns to prioritize meaningful and positive experiences. Stopping to notice and celebrate small wins isn't self-indulgent; it is the most neurologically responsible thing you can do for your brain and the kindest thing you can do for yourself. Seeing your progress is one of the most often cited vitality ignitors, not to mention a powerful way to spark the motivation and energy to keep going when you have a long road ahead.

What Self-Compassion Is and Isn't

Kristin Neff, a pioneering researcher on self-compassion and the cofounder of the Center for Mindful Self-Compassion, shares that there are three elements to self-compassion: self-kindness, mindfulness, and common humanity.

Self-kindness means using kinder, more supportive words and thoughts instead of bullying yourself with harsh self-judgment and criticism. It is practiced by simply being a friend to yourself. A good best friend asks you what you need, has your back, tells it like it is, and supports you in a productive and helpful way. I guarantee you already know how to do this for others, so now focus that skill on yourself.

Mindfulness can simply be thought of as the act of paying attention and being present in the moment. When it comes to emotions, mindfulness helps you to experience emotions, particularly difficult ones, without avoiding, exaggerating, or overpersonalizing them. It helps you to take ownership where appropriate, let go when needed, and to persevere without getting lost in difficult emotions. As you explore stress in the next section, you'll dive deeper into how to work with difficult emotions mindfully.

And lastly, finding a sense of *common humanity* means acknowledging that suffering and failure are part of being human, not something uniquely dysfunctional about you personally, but an experience shared by us all.

Self-compassion isn't about lowering the bar on your standards or letting yourself off the hook. It is about learning that it's okay to struggle and giving yourself the space to improve. It's about learning to celebrate the small wins without discounting yourself or moving the goalpost. It is about interpreting your failures and successes in a realistic, level-headed, less perfectionist way. This is how you learn to have your own back. Enough things out there smother your vitality; don't be among them.

Keisha, the Self-Compassionate CFO

As we worked together, Keisha realized that the deficit of vitality she felt in her work wasn't a result of her ambition; it was due to her exhausting and endless pursuit of perfection. Her ever-rising standards kept her from truly enjoying the process or feeling satisfied with herself or her accomplishments. Building up her Work Vitality Quotient started with exploring self-compassion and the scientific evidence of its impact on health, well-being, and performance. The more she did, the deeper her commitment became to practicing it.

Balancing your high
standards with
self-compassion fuels
your best work.

Instead of acting on outdated beliefs driven by fear, obligation, and guilt, as well as accepting that everything didn't have to be so hard, meant Keisha discovered she could feel more joy, ease, and fulfillment pursuing success in her work. But perhaps the biggest insight was when she realized that she'd excelled all these years—not because of her unrealistic perfectionistic standards—but despite them.

Keisha decided to pass up the CFO job in the end. Not because she doubted her ability, but because the organization she worked for had a culture of toxic overwork. She did, however, stay with the organization for a couple of more years, taking that time to redefine how she thought about and pursued success. She started intentionally applying practices to create a healthier and more sustainable balance between life and work. She shared those changes openly with her organization, helping to create positive shifts in the culture. She also took a ten-day cruise, unplugging from work for the first time in twelve years.

A couple of years later, she accepted a CFO position with another organization, bringing her self-compassion to the role. Does she feel exhausted at times? Absolutely. Is her work stressful and demanding? That is putting it mildly. And she'll be the first to tell you that she is a work in progress when it comes to balancing ambition and excellence with self-compassion.

But rather than trying to be a perfect role model, now Keisha focuses on being an empowering leader and a healthy role model, and believes she is doing the best work of her life.

Instead of believing that holding yourself to the highest standard fuels your best work, the updated work relationship belief that strengthens your Work Vitality Quotient is that balancing your high standards with self-compassion fuels your best work.

Dear Stress,

do I really need to
break up with you?

9

Getting Better at Stress

IN 2012, Tim Kreider wrote a now-legendary piece for the
New York Times, "The 'Busy' Trap," highlighting our culture's
obsession with busyness. Over a decade later, we're still
wearing busyness like a badge of honor, but with the onset
of the 2020 pandemic, the emphasis changed. Now when most
people are asked how they are doing, the typical response of "I'm
so busy!" has been replaced by "I'm so stressed!" Whether people
are worried, tired, overwhelmed, frustrated, feeling blue, bored, or
even busy, "stress" is now the catch-all word to describe everything
we feel and experience that we don't like and have too much of in
our lives. Stress isn't just a part of our lives anymore; being stressed
seems to have become a way of life.

Stress has been dubbed the "health epidemic of the 21st century"
by the World Health Organization, and internet searches related
to the word "stress" have steadily increased over the last decade.
According to Google's internal metrics, in 2021, "why do I feel sad?"
was searched more times than ever before—a 10 percent increase
from 2020. Search results for this question offer strategies to tame,

combat, and cope with stress, including step-by-step methods for living a stress-free life. It makes sense, considering how rarely we talk about stress in a positive way.

Although most people appreciate that short, manageable doses of stress can be good, most also believe that even this "good stress" becomes bad if there's too much of it, it happens too often, or it goes on for too long. When it comes to our beliefs about the nature of stress in general, we tend to believe that less stress should be the goal.

There's no disputing the mountains of scientific evidence documenting the negative outcomes associated with stress which would support this belief. It absolutely can hijack your thinking and in the wrong context can diminish your Work Vitality Quotient and keep you spinning your wheels in the survival zone.

Understanding stress and its influence on workplace dynamics as well as individually on our health, relationships, well-being, and performance is essential. So is understanding the ripple effect stress can have when considering how to tackle some of our world's most pressing problems, such as mental health, financial inequity, and social injustice, to name just a few. The urgency of addressing stress and its impact is warranted. That is also precisely why it is imperative to recognize that our beliefs about stress and how we approach it might be as much of the problem as is the stress we face.

There is a growing body of research in the fields of psychology and neuroscience that suggests seeing stress as the core of our problems only increases the risk of feeling hopeless, overwhelmed, and exhausted by it. And while it is likely contrary to what you may believe in this moment, when it comes to boosting your Work Vitality Quotient, the solution isn't about combating bad stress or leveraging good stress, it's letting go of the lens of "good stress and bad stress" and instead aiming to get better at addressing and working with stress in general.

When Only Good Stress Is Good
. . . .

While it may not be automatically apparent, there are significant consequences to separating good stress from bad. For example, when you read the words "good stress," what do you think of? Most people associate good stress with positive life-changing events, such as getting married, having children, and getting a promotion. Others describe a thrilling experience such as skiing a black diamond run or engaging in something outside of their comfort zone; something that helps them learn, grow, and even conquer a fear.

What about in the workplace? When is stress "good"? What usually follows are people's descriptions of when stress helps their performance—when their stress-response system is activated just enough to be both manageable and motivating. Others describe high-pressure situations when teams come together around a shared purpose to meet a deadline. Or high-risk/high-reward moments where the fear of failure is matched with a sense of excitement and possibility.

It's not a mystery how to generate more of these experiences. A 7,500-person survey by Gallup found that employees are less likely to burn out when the following criteria are met: they have a manager they trust, who inspires them, and who has their back; when the work culture feels fair and psychologically safe; and where workloads are manageable, timelines are reasonable, and roles, responsibilities, and priorities are clear.

Can we just pause for a moment to acknowledge that *of course* we see stress as being good when it helps us perform, it's highly rewarding, and when it is built on trust, safety, and clarity. These are the conditions where we feel most alive precisely because they set us up to be successful, making it easy to work from our standout zone. While these are desirable experiences and environments to aim for, I also have a hunch that rarely is this how you'd describe the stress you encounter and the culture you work in on a day-to-day basis. While workplace culture is a significant contributor to burnout, that doesn't mean a healthy culture is stress-free, nor should we want it to be.

For starters, humans are complex, unique, and imperfect and since our workplaces are made up of humans, they will be as well. We'll always cause each other stress because we have diverse ideologies, cultural expectations, approaches, experiences, and skill sets. And while inarguably difficult to navigate, those are the same aspects that contribute to innovative and inclusive outcomes.

Add to this, having a narrow range for what we consider "good stress" means most of our experiences are going to fall outside of these parameters, making the possibility of raising our Work Vitality Quotient *feel* impossible.

I'm not suggesting taking the onus off organizations to create more supportive workplace cultures. Nor should we stop striving to make things better. Rather, if you are committed to boosting your Work Vitality Quotient, you can't make it contingent on working within an ideal environment faced with the ideal type of stress. There are two core reasons for this:

- Because, in all my work, I have yet to meet a team or workplace where all these ideal elements are present all the time.

- Because rarely do you get to choose your stress, including how much of it you experience, how long it lasts, and how supported you feel through it.

You may be thinking to yourself, "Does it really matter how you label stress if the end goal is to lessen it regardless?" The short answer is no—if your goal is just to get rid of stress. The challenge is, it's exactly that thinking that makes stress so difficult, and the vitality that you are seeking feel so out of reach.

When Stress Is Mostly Bad

"That's it, I am swearing off of dating!" This is a text I received from a friend following a string of bad dates. And while the online dating

While workplace culture is a significant contributor to burnout, a healthy culture is not stress-free, nor should we want it to be.

world can seem like the modern-day wild west, such a sweeping approach meant my friend was potentially cutting themselves off from the committed, loving relationship they deeply longed for. While I'm sure we'd advise our friends against this approach, when it comes to stress, we tend to take the same all-or-nothing stance, focusing on the negatives and swearing off it all.

When you generally see stress as something bad, it follows that your decisions, behaviors, and coping mechanisms are geared toward either getting rid of it or protecting yourself from its negative consequences. Given what you know about your brain's design, it's natural to gravitate toward strategies that help you feel *less stressed*: to dial stress down, work around it, or eliminate it altogether.

On the surface such strategies may even seem to provide moments of relief and help you through short periods of stress. Unfortunately, these same strategies are rarely sustainable in the long run. Instead, they tend to worsen or even add new sources of stress rather than alleviate it. Perhaps most dishearteningly, dial-down, work-around, or elimination strategies often take you further away from the goals you care about the most and the vitality you so deeply desire.

I have spent a great deal of time coaching leaders, and unsurprisingly, stress often tops the list of things they want to change. I have noticed five popular stress coping mechanisms, self-protective in nature, that inadvertently keep people feeling stuck in the survival zone versus freeing them from it:

- Distraction

- Daydreaming

- Dwelling

- Denial

- Directing

Before exploring each of these in detail, it is important to note that we all default into one or more of these at times. Not because we're flawed people who are doing "life" wrong. But because life can be hard, and we are human beings trying to do the best we can with what we know and the resources we have available. And that's the power. If you learn to recognize these coping strategies when you're doing them, whether they are protective, defensive, or avoidant in nature, then you can choose to do something different and improve your ability to "do stress" overall and work more consistently from your stand-out zone.

Distraction

You have a huge deadline coming up, and you're kicking yourself for not starting earlier. Before settling in for a couple of hours of work, you decide to change into something more comfortable. Opening the closet, you're suddenly struck by an overwhelming need to reorganize and finally get rid of all the hangers that don't match. Thirty minutes later—after the hanger switch—you sit back at your desk. As you get started, you wonder if you should run to the store to buy some new colored Post-it notes to help organize things... or do these experiences only describe me?

We've all gotten caught up by distraction and its best friend, procrastination. While it's tempting to think the answer lies in the latest time management strategy or goal-setting journal, Tim Pychyl, member of the Procrastination Research Group at Carleton University, shared in a *New York Times* article that distraction and procrastination are less a problem of time management (though this does matter) and more a problem with emotional regulation.

When faced with complex situations and the uncomfortable emotions they can provoke, including feeling anxious, bored, overwhelmed, uncertain, or dread of an upcoming task or event, your brain tries to alleviate these feelings with an easier, safer, and immediately rewarding distraction.

This makes sense since distractions provide relief in the form of a feel-good dopamine hit. However, it's not the distraction itself that triggers the dopamine release, which is why simply locking yourself in a distraction-free room doesn't mean you'll be focused and productive. It is the *emotional anticipation* of there being a reward from that distraction that triggers the dopamine release. This helps explain why your brain can convince you that once you do that one thing that's pulling on your attention, *then* you'll feel better and be ready to work. As we all know, this is almost never the case.

Unfortunately, the actual distraction is rarely as rewarding as anticipated and whatever relief you experienced is typically short-lived, leaving you no further ahead on your project but more self-critical and regretful of the time lost. Judson Brewer, author of *Unwinding Anxiety*, calls this the *anxiety-distraction loop*. The longer you cycle through the loop, the less likely you are to address the source of your stress.

Instead of allowing a restless mind and uncomfortable feelings to pull you off course, stop and check in. Ask yourself what feels hard, and be as specific as possible. And then think of the smallest step you can take to address it. Instead of the dopamine hit coming from the distraction, it will come in anticipation of the small win of moving toward your goal.

Daydreaming

"Wouldn't it be nice if there was an easy button for life?" This was the slogan of a wildly successful Staples advertising campaign. The ads depicted a series of challenging scenarios, none of which appeared to have any simple solution. Hence the easy button: just push it, and all becomes easy. The ad was popular because it was relatable. Who hasn't found themselves daydreaming about an easy button to provide a clean, quick fix to all life's problems?

But sometimes it's more than an easy answer that you desire; it's an escape button to eject yourself out of your current circumstances and leave your stress behind. The number of times I have had people confess that they fantasized about being in an accident in which they needed to be hospitalized for a few weeks, just to escape life's stress, is staggering.

While a little daydreaming doesn't hurt, when dreams become fantasies that delude you into believing you're one big change away from a different life where everything will be okay is when things become dangerous and regrettable decisions get made. Instead, use daydreaming as a signal that you need to confront something hard. Ask for help from others and make a real plan to work through your challenges instead of feeling ashamed and guilty for having such thoughts in the first place.

Dwelling

"I've lived through some terrible things in my life, some of which actually happened." This quote, attributed to Mark Twain, perfectly captures dwelling, which occurs when people overfocus on problems and potentially negative outcomes, including those that haven't even happened yet.

Strategizing about the future, reflecting on the past, and self-examination are all helpful when the end result is to gain additional clarity on your goals, consider new perspectives, and brainstorm potential solutions. In contrast, dwelling is thinking about a problem or potential problem but never moving on. It can take the form of overthinking, ruminating, or letting your internal critic take over. Dwelling is often a result of the brain's negativity bias in overdrive.

On the surface, dwelling appears to be the opposite of avoidance, since you're focused on nothing but the stress-inducing problem, but it actually serves to avoid *solutions*. Studies show the more you analyze and scrutinize the same information, the more distorted your interpretation of the details becomes. Your dwelled-upon versions of events are often riddled with self-criticism, judgment, and blame. Your worries feel more dire, your options feel more limited, and you are less likely to take action on the learning or insight available. As we'll dive into more deeply in the pages ahead, stress is designed to move you into action; therefore, it helps to remember that analysis without action is a breeding ground for anxiety.

Denial

If you want to change someone's mind, all you need to do is present facts, right? Unfortunately, when faced with a situation that has the potential to turn someone's worldview upside down, the first line of defense is the ultimate avoidance strategy, denial.

While rarely discussed in a positive light, denial is a natural, self-protective response to difficult situations. Following an unexpected and emotionally jarring event or realization, often the first stage of processing is denial. It is meant to be a short stop on the path to working through difficult situations. When it takes up residence as a coping mechanism, it becomes a problem.

Denial can take on the forms of ignoring, dismissing, or resisting problems. Alternatively, people may acknowledge the problem but then discount or downplay their role or ability to do something about it. You can hear denial in action with statements like:

"It's fine. Just leave it alone!"

"What's the point? Nothing will change anyway."

"Relax, you're making a big deal about nothing."

"It's not a problem; I've got it under control."

There is a difference between not sweating the small stuff and denying the bad stuff. I recall a gentleman I met while teaching an executive education program who claimed to hate his job—"soul-sucking" was how he described it. When asked why he stayed, he said he didn't think he could afford the pay cut required to take the job he actually wanted because his daughter had special needs and her support services were expensive. He committed to looking into options, including his current expenses and a budget that would financially allow him to take a job he enjoyed more and still support his daughter. Weeks later, when the group was back together, I heard someone complimenting him on his new luxury car. "The other job probably wouldn't work out, so since I'm stuck, I might as well enjoy driving to the job I hate." Unfortunately, denial is often accompanied by a victim mindset. After all, it's easier to blame your circumstances and other people then it is to take ownership of your choices and reactions.

The consequence of denial is it often leads to unaddressed problems spiraling out of control while the pool of helpful solutions dwindles. As a result, though difficult to admit, we create our own prisons while we deny we're the ones who hold the key.

Directing

Sometimes a stress-avoidance strategy can look like positive coping; directing is one such strategy. Directing looks like going into action-overdrive, which often presents itself as hyper-focusing on detailed plans, rigid structure, and limiting emotions.

"Directors" are your take-over-and-create-order people. Although directing can initially provide clarity to tackle stressful, anxiety-provoking situations, the motivation is centered on creating a sense of control, even over uncontrollable things, such as circumstances, the future, and other people. When using a directing coping mechanism, you convince yourself that the more structure you have, the harder you hold on to things, the more you can keep the bad stuff at bay. Unfortunately, this thinking leaves you feeling restricted and unfulfilled because all your energy is invested in holding it together. To the outside world, you look self-reliant when really, you feel one crisis away from imploding.

There is a fine line between emotional regulation and emotional suppression. Emotional regulation is about acknowledging emotions and the information they provide without letting your feelings overwhelm you. You process them and express them intentionally, appropriately, and safely. The emotions get felt, get acknowledged, and then get addressed. When it comes to directing, suppressing emotions means you push down uncomfortable and overwhelming emotions in attempts to make them more manageable. Any benefit of this approach, however, is short-lived on three counts.

First, actively suppressing emotions is exhausting. Second, a study from the University of Texas found that attempting to resist emotions only makes them stronger and prolongs your experience of them. Third, suppressing emotions doesn't get rid of them; it diverts them. Because of this, you increase the likelihood of an outburst like snapping at your spouse, being brisk with a grocery clerk, or allow-ing an entire night to be ruined when you internally transform into the green-skinned Hulk if your delivery order comes without the guacamole that you paid extra for. Let's be honest, it's never about the guacamole; it's the pent-up emotion that needed an outlet.

While each of these responses is understandable and human, the more you see feeling stress as an indication that something is wrong with negative consequences, the more likely you are to reach for avoidance-based strategies.

Forced, False, Unrealistic Positivity

"We love stress here because we know that it's through good stress that we grow." This was a conversation I had with the leader of a tech start-up firm. He went on to say, "This is a very stressful envi-ronment, so to combat that, our number one value is positivity." He then proceeded to recite their positivity manifesto: "We don't accept negative vibes, only positivity. We don't focus on obstacles; we find opportunities. And we look at adversity as a gift we simply haven't opened yet."

Sounds great on paper, right? But this leader's people were burned out and leaving, so something wasn't working. It seems that if we're not focused on feeling shortchanged on good stress or talking about how to get out from under the thumb of bad stress, we're trying to paint a happy face on top of it.

While keeping a positive frame of mind, including feeling hope-ful, optimistic, and confident, is helpful when you face a stressful event, it is rarely a complete representation of the emotions you experience. In a culture that values positivity above all else, nega-tive feelings can feel inappropriate, which becomes a slippery slope into what is known as toxic positivity.

Positivity becomes toxic when forced on people to the point of feeling false and unrealistic given the circumstances. For example, positivity can be toxic when:

- It makes people feel obligated to immediately bounce back or brush things off by putting on a brave face regardless of the circumstances.

- It trivializes people's experiences by comparing them to those who "have it worse," making them feel guilty for struggling.

- Perhaps most damaging, it makes people fear that if they share their struggles, they'll be seen as weak or be labeled a "Debbie Downer" or "Gloomy Gus," a complainer or attention seeker.

This approach is what Susan David, author of *Emotional Agility*, calls the tyranny of positivity. She shares, "Once we stop struggling to eliminate distressing feelings or to smother them with positive affirmations and rationalizations, they can teach us valuable lessons." In other words, when we try to get rid of the uncomfortable and hard emotions that come with stress, we hinder our capacity to build the skills and confidence to deal with them in the future.

Now, I am embarrassed to admit that, while I am critical of the "good vibes only" mentality, I too find myself inadvertently crossing over into the land of toxic positivity. My husband has described me as the "gratitude police."

In 2019, my husband had started a tourism-focused event. His goal wasn't to build a for-profit business, but a self-sustaining set of events to create experiences and education for people around the craft beer industry. It was an intrinsically motivated creative outlet for him.

On the heels of a very successful event, he was excited and ready to expand the concept. Then the pandemic hit, and all in-person group events were restricted. Each time he'd be down, disappointed, or upset, I'd jump in to remind him how lucky he was. It was a hobby, and he could start again after the pandemic. He should be grateful he had a job and that our circumstances allowed us to experience the pandemic differently than so many others.

One day, he said, "I know it could be worse! You just need to let me be disappointed and sad about it anyway." He was right. I was

When we see
stress as the enemy,
vitality becomes an
inadvertent casualty.

not only discounting how he felt by comparing his experience to others, but I was guilting him into feeling grateful and being positive while simultaneously trying to control how I believed he should express his thoughts and feelings.

The line between positive encouragement and attitudes and toxic positivity can sometimes seem blurry. Although often well intentioned, a simple rule of thumb is that if you make yourself or someone else feel bad for feeling bad, then toxic positivity is likely at play.

At its root, toxic positivity is a consolidation of avoidance-based strategies, stamped with a smile. It is a denial of reality, an attempt at directing and suppressing genuine emotions. It is daydreaming about how we wish things were and using distractions to make us feel better and create the "positive" feeling we believe we need to have.

Stress and Your Work Vitality Quotient

While we often perceive stress as something that drains us, when it comes to strengthening our Work Vitality Quotient it can also be something that guides us. After all, we feel most alive when aligned with what matters.

In her bestselling book *The Upside of Stress*, Kelly McGonigal defines stress as what arises in us when something that matters to us feels at stake. While our brain desires comfort, vitality is generated in part through the pursuit and accomplishment of meaningful goals and experiences, which often involves doing hard and uncomfortable things and taking the scarier path. As such, experiencing stress is a non-negotiable aspect of that journey—vitality and stress are directly connected. The problem is our traditional approach is to see stress as the enemy. But when we hold this perspective, vitality becomes the inadvertent casualty.

McGonigal brilliantly writes about the mounting body of research making the case that now more than ever it is vital to recognize that viewing stress as solely harmful only increases the risk of feeling overwhelmed and powerless in the face of it. She and other research-ers are showing that embracing stress can make you more resilient, confident, and energized. When it comes to cultivating vitality, this is certainly the case.

What is clear is that the way we typically approach stress is not supporting our goals and desires, and, as it turns out, it doesn't support our Work Vitality Quotient either. Instead of stress repre-senting everything you don't want, you will learn that stress is an important and non-negotiable element in the generation of vitality when you learn to work with it in a meaningful and healthy way.

10

Using a "Yes, and" Stress Mindset

I T HAD been a long week. Scratch that; it had been a long
quarter. Sandy's team was in the final stages of launching a
new product. The success of this project depended on a positive collaboration between Sandy's R&D group and Tom's
sales and marketing team. That collaboration had not blossomed
as hoped.

Sandy and Tom had different working styles. Being decisive
and action-oriented, Sandy found indecision incredibly frustrating.
Unfortunately, Tom tended to waver on decisions. In meetings,
Tom would enthusiastically agree with decisions, only to send an
email a day later with his concerns, requesting they reconsider. The
cycle became so common and frustrating that Sandy's team began
to refer to him as "Triggering Tom."

Things came to boil one winter day. After sitting in back-to-back
meetings all morning and the afternoon looking like more of the
same, Sandy attempted to use the short break in between to address
her overflowing inbox. She and her team had met with Tom the

125

day before to confirm final launch details. Tom had enthusiastically backed the plan, but as Sandy scanned her inbox, she saw an email from Tom. "Of course, a Triggering Tom email!" Sandy mockingly said out loud to her computer. Opening the email it read:

Sandy,

I'm sorry you didn't have this information sooner but seeing as you haven't spoken with the sales team directly, I wanted you to see their concerns about the launch. You might want to reconsider your strategy. I'd hate to see this go wrong so late in the game.

Before she even finished the email, thoughts began rushing through Sandy's mind, starting with, "Are you kidding me? You aren't sorry, Tom!" Followed by variations of, "Are you seriously insinuating I haven't done my due diligence to get feedback from YOUR team?" Which then escalated into, "You'd love to see this go wrong, Tom!"

At that moment, Sandy felt certain that this wasn't just a case of Tom's indecision; this was Tom intentionally discrediting Sandy's leadership and sabotaging the launch. Even as Sandy's rational mind told her that she should calm down before responding, she hit reply, ready to fire back an email in response.

And then she stopped. Not because it was the right thing to do, but because she realized the reply was going to Hank. Momentarily confused, she scrolled down to reread the original message, which clarified the problem. In her rush to see what "Triggering Tom" had to say, she'd accidentally clicked on the email *below* Tom's, which meant that the email Sandy had just read and was about to respond to wasn't from Tom; it was from Hank, one of her most trusted and helpful colleagues who happened to work directly with the sales team.

While the email was still stressful and frustrating, Sandy's anger instantly shifted to concern and consideration as she thoroughly reread the contents of the email recognizing the value of the information. Not a single word had changed, but Sandy's mindset had.

Your mindset
shapes how you
make sense of the
world and, in turn,
respond to it.

Mindsets Matter
....

You see the term "mindset" used often and not always in the same way, so let's agree on a definition: think of a mindset like a filter you view experiences through, shaping how you make sense of the world and respond to it.

When Sandy first read the email, it was through a "Triggering Tom" mindset, so she interpreted the information in general as harmful, which led her to believe Tom intended to sabotage her and the launch. But when she read it through the "Helpful Hank" mindset, suddenly the message wasn't about undermining her; it was about supporting her. Helpful Hank's words of warning weren't meant to put her down, they were meant to set her up for success. Asking Sandy to reconsider her plan was a sign of having her back, not discrediting her leadership.

Stress Mindsets
....

Years of research have shown that your mindset fundamentally shifts how you see the world, which, in turn, influences your perceptions, decisions, and actions. Perhaps the most powerful research finding on mindsets is that you can change them if they do not serve you.

Recognizing the malleability and influence of mindsets on people's lives drew the attention of researchers Alia Crum, Peter Salovey, and Shawn Achor. While most researchers were studying ways to minimize stress and lessen its damaging effects, Crum and her colleagues wondered if our mindsets about the nature of stress influenced the impact stress had on us. More specifically, could our widespread tendency to focus on the undesirable and harmful effects of stress be making its debilitating outcomes more likely? If so, could expanding our perspective to include the positive and enhancing effects of stress in turn make those helpful outcomes more likely?

The researchers devised a set of studies that tested how holding a negative mindset toward stress (a stress-is-debilitating mindset;

i.e., stress is harmful and should be eliminated) differed as compared to those holding a mindset about the enhancing benefits (a stress-is-enhancing mindset; i.e., stress is important and can be helpful). The initial set of results was unequivocal: our beliefs about the nature of stress in general and therefore our stress mindset makes a difference in how we experience stress and the consequences it has on our performance, health, and well-being.

Now, a caveat: a stress-is-enhancing mindset is not meant to negate negative stressors such as grief, poverty, racism, abuse, disease, and toxic workplaces. Nor does it deny the potentially negative outcomes of severe and chronic stress. Rather it highlights an important point: stress is made of two elements. The stressor, or the thing that provoked the stress response, and the actual stress response. While the stressor may be bad, not all outcomes of that stressor are necessarily negative. As we'll explore further, embracing a fuller perspective of stress can contribute to living a more meaningful life in the long run.

Stress Can Be Helpful and Enhancing

In the spring of 2021, I ran a survey in partnership with a business association. Their goal was to get a better understanding of the stress levels their members were facing and the challenges stress was creating. Before distributing it, I suggested adding some questions focusing on the following evidence-based benefits of stress:

- Clarifying values and priorities

- Strengthening relationships

- Increased adaptability

- Deeper appreciation and gratitude

- Heightened sense of purposefulness and meaning

Although skeptical, they agreed. As expected, members reported back high levels of stress. But to the association's surprise, of the nearly thousand survey respondents, well over half also reported experiencing the beneficial outcomes as well. This group was not an anomaly; I suspect you may have had similar experiences.

Taking on a stress-is-enhancing mindset isn't about trying to trick yourself into seeing stress as good, nor is it predicated on being solely positive. It is about expanding your perspective to include more of the science around stress and the benefits it can produce. For example, stress-related growth is a phenomenon in which an individual is fundamentally changed for the better following an intensely negative experience. In addition to the examples listed above, other positive benefits that influence health, well-being, and performance include the development of enhanced efficacy, mental toughness, self-confidence, self-awareness, and an increased propensity to volunteer and engage in hard but meaningful experiences.

One study found that oscillating cycles of stress followed by rest increased learning and memory and resulted in a more robustly connected brain, as compared to test subjects that weren't challenged by stress. While this study's subjects were mice, multiple studies show representative brain activity and enhanced performance when people experience the same cycles of stress and recovery.

While most people acknowledge that these are potential outcomes, perhaps the biggest obstacle in shifting our beliefs about the enhancing effects of stress is centered on what we've learned about the fight-or-flight response.

Stress Is More Than Fight-or-Flight

As someone who studies and teaches in the fields of leadership, resilience, and emotional intelligence, I can tell you that rarely is stress associated with people being at their best. The common teaching is that when you are triggered by a negative event—big or small, important or not—your fight-or-flight system kicks in, leading to a set of unsophisticated and often extreme reactions.

While such reactions might be beneficial if your life is on the line, rarely are they seen as helpful if you're on a videoconference call with your boss. In other words, the standard message is that your stress response is an outdated survival mechanism that hasn't evolved to keep up with modern-day demands. As such, we blame stress for many of our undesirable behaviors, and as a result, approach stress as something to wrangle in to prevent it from working against us.

There is no argument that the impact of your fight-or-flight stress response can be detrimental if your life is not on the line. It's that, contrary to popular belief, the fight-or-flight response isn't the *only* stress response you have.

Whenever you face a stressful situation, your brain weighs the perceived demands of the situation against the resources you bring to it and rapidly assesses your ability to handle it. When the demands are too large or your brain feels unequipped or under-resourced to handle them, a threat response is generated, initiating your fight-or-flight response. However, the more you see the demands as an opportunity to connect to what is meaningful in the situation, and/or the more capable and resourceful you feel to deal with demands, the more likely you'll produce a challenge-based stress response.

Whereas fight-or-flight puts you in self-protective, *get-through-it mode*, a challenge-based stress response often invokes a take-it-on and *get-better-because-of-it response*. Depending on the situation, different types of challenge-based stress responses are possible. Kelly McGonigal, health psychologist, lecturer at Stanford, and author of the book *The Upside of Stress*, which I referenced in the last chapter, describes a number of challenge-based stress responses that you can intentionally draw on. Although you may not realize it, you already use most, if not all, of these responses.

Your Repertoire of Challenge-Based Stress Responses

Let me prove it to you. Think back to the years 2020 and 2021. Those years, most people experienced one or many of the following: anxiety, disappointment, grief, loneliness, fear, anger, or a sense of generalized "blah." Instead of succumbing to these feelings, think about specific examples where you responded in one or more of the following ways:

- You focused on what you were learning and how you could grow from the experience.

- You reached out to others to share your struggles, to ask for help or to offer it.

- You joined a cause to contribute to something bigger than you alone could change.

- You tackled something head-on, even though it would have been easier not to.

- You allowed yourself to slow down, not act, and instead reflect, recalibrate, and plan.

These challenge-based responses still create physiological sensations within the body but have a markedly different physiological response compared with a threat response. The impact is much healthier and more helpful.

For example, during a fight-or-flight threat response your blood vessels constrict; however, when you see something as a meaningful opportunity to learn and grow, or rise to the challenge, your blood vessels relax and open. Instead of your heart needing to work hard, increasing blood pressure with a threat response, with a challenge response your heart beats more strongly, forcefully, and efficiently, giving you more energy without the unhealthy cardiac impact. Instead of being reactive and amygdala-driven, a challenge response is more considered because it is prefrontal cortex driven.

Your Stress Growth Index

In the same way that we often only associate flight-or-fight when we think about our stress response, we also tend to exclusively think of cortisol as the main hormone. While cortisol is a stress *response* hormone, we also have stress *recovery* hormones. One of particular relevance is DHEA (dehydroepiandrosterone). As a recovery hormone, DHEA helps to both protect and counteract the wear-and-tear effects of cortisol, particularly in the brain.

While the presence of DHEA helps with recovery, the level of it has been shown to have stress-enhancing effects. Specifically, the ratio of DHEA levels to cortisol levels is known as the Stress Growth Index. When DHEA is higher than cortisol, a positive Stress Growth Index is achieved. Not only does this buffer the brain from the negative effects of stress, but it also strengthens it by explicitly leveraging the neurological changes prompted by stress to help us learn and build resilience for the future. This process is known as psychological thriving and is a direct outcome uniquely experienced as a result of stress.

A "Yes, and" Mindset toward Stress

In a 2020 *School of Greatness* podcast, Kelly McGonigal shared a powerful improv metaphor to understand—and access—the stress-is-enhancing mindset described by Alia Crum and her colleagues. One of the foundations of improv is a technique known as "yes, and..." or the acceptance principle. One improvisor shares an idea, and their partner's job is to accept by saying "yes" and build on it with the word "and" to expand the possibilities, including the paradoxes, to carry the scene forward.

While toxic positivity is about dismissing or ignoring the negatives of a situation, the "yes" of the stress-enhancing mindset *accepts* that stress can be detrimental, difficult, uncomfortable, anxiety-provoking, as well as energy-taxing on our health, relationships, well-being, and performance. The "and" broadens that perspective to *include* the evidence-backed data that shows stress can also create psychological thriving and be life-enhancing, helping us to

A "yes, and"
stress mindset accepts
the negatives and
expands your
perspective to include
the benefits stress
can generate.

achieve goals, create a meaningful life, and be our best, healthiest, and most resilient selves.

The Application of a "Yes, and" Stress Mindset

The work of Crum and others is compelling and broad. To establish the value of shifting your beliefs about the nature of stress and embracing a "yes, and" stress mindset as a crucial strategy in boosting your Work Vitality Quotient, I am going to extrapolate some key findings and apply them to a fictitious situation.

Imagine yourself in the following scenario. You've been a part of a team preparing a pitch for two new potential clients. Getting these clients would be a great win for the company. On the day of the presentation, the lead on the project has an unexpected family emergency and cannot attend. You have been volunteered—or more like "voluntold"—that you will need to fill in and deliver the two presentations. Gulp!

To clear your head, you pop in your earphones and go for a walk, listening to your favorite podcast, which happens to be a series on the nature of stress and associated strategies.

That afternoon you nervously head into your first presentation and are met by the client's decision-making lead and their team. The client smiles, nods along, and openly validates your ideas as you present. They share constructive feedback on your pitch and their concerns about going with your company. Even in the face of that tough feedback, you feel confident and capable afterward.

Following a short break, you head into your second presentation. Again, you are met by the client lead, but unlike with your first pitch, this client is standoffish and abrupt. As you start to present, they shake their head, roll their eyes, and sigh multiple times, looking at their phone. If that isn't bad enough, they criticize your approach and dismiss your ideas and company. You feel as if you've been thrown to the wolves and can't get out of the room fast enough.

We've all been in situations where we feel judged by others, whether when speaking up in a meeting, interviewing for a job, or in an awkward social situation. In such situations, your response to stress matters, not just for your performance within the moment but because our lives and work are full of stressful situations. While you can't always control the stress you face, you can choose the mindset you take toward stress in general to help you bring your best to the moment.

Turning your attention back to the fictitious scenario, in the first presentation to the engaging client you would expect this would most likely elicit more of a challenge stress response, whereas the second presentation to the dismissive, combative client would almost definitely activate your threat-based, fight-or-flight response. The real question is, based on Crum's research, how do your beliefs about the general nature of stress affect your reactions to these situations?

Stress *Is* Hard

While factors such as experience, expertise, and perceived power differences, as well as general health and well-being, will influence things, there is bad news when it comes to stress. It turns out that, regardless of your stress mindset, when you have skin in the game, or there is an element of uncertainty as to the success of the outcome, or you feel socially judged, stress is stressful!

Stress increases the presence of negative and uncomfortable emotions, such as apprehension, fear, and self-doubt, and as a result rarely feels enjoyable in the moment. Additionally, cortisol levels typically increase. Although perhaps more so presenting to the dismissive client versus the engaging one, either way stress physiologically taxes the body. The bottom line is that stress is hard, and we need recovery periods to allow the body to move through the stress cycle to buffer these effects.

But there is good news as well. If you had been listening to a podcast focused on the *enhancing outcomes* associated with stress and as a result, embraced a "yes, and" stress mindset, the potential helpful aspects of stress would improve, and the hard elements of stress would get healthier.

The Benefits of Stress Get Better with a "Yes, and" Stress Mindset

Unfortunately, a "yes, and" stress mindset doesn't mean you'll stop being nervous, self-critical, or overthinking—I wish it were that easy! True to the nature of the "yes, and" improv principle: *yes*, you will experience negative and uncomfortable emotions during the presentation, *and* there is also an increased likelihood you will experience positive emotions following the presentation. You are more likely to put negative emotions and stressors into perspective and bounce back more quickly. You are more likely to extract the learning from situations more readily to build skills, confidence, and resilience while also having the energy available to approach the next difficult situation.

This holds true even when presenting to the dismissive client who likely triggered your fight-or-flight response. With a "yes, and" stress mindset, you can move on more quickly from the difficult thoughts and emotions and still feel energized, capable, and resourceful after. Finally, embracing a "yes, and" stress mindset regardless of the client you face makes your challenge-based stress responses easier to access and therefore benefit from, even in difficult moments.

The Hard Elements of Stress Get Healthier with a "Yes, and" Stress Mindset

We know that cortisol levels will rise regardless of the client you present to, but holding a "yes, and" stress mindset tends to elicit a greater Stress Growth Index, meaning higher DHEA levels as compared to cortisol levels. As importantly, both hormones will tend to drop back to baseline levels more quickly. Not only does this suggest a faster completion of the stress cycle and less wear-and-tear on the body, but a potentially strengthening effect as a result of a positive Stress Growth Index.

If You Believe Stress Is Debilitating, It Will Be

Now the kicker. In our imagined scenario, if you had been listening to a podcast series focused on all the ways stress was harmful and you walked into the presentation with a stress-is-debilitating mindset—even when presenting to the *engaging client*—you would likely still experience a negative Stress Growth Index. Add to this, fewer positive emotions and more focus on the negative elements long after the presentation. The inability to disengage from negative emotions and thoughts is one reason your stress response stays engaged long after the actual stressful event has occurred, which is why holding a stress-is-debilitating mindset when facing a stressful situation is so emotionally exhausting. As a result, you are left feeling drained by an event that could have been a positive experience.

When you are presenting to the *dismissive client*, on top of the negative Stress Growth Index, when holding a stress-is-debilitating mindset, hormone levels would also take longer to restabilize, increasing the negative physiological effects of stress. Overall, the demands of the presentation would feel more menacing, and you would likely feel less capable and resourceful to handle them. You'd probably dwell on the negatives longer and experience fewer positive emotions after, altogether making stress feel more frustrating and exhausting. In other words, regardless of the situation, if you label it stressful *all of the negative effects of stress that you expected to happen, will happen when you hold a stress-is-debilitating mindset.*

This is why it matters how we talk about stress. Focusing so narrowly on the negatives reinforces the belief that stress is solely harmful regardless of the circumstances. In turn, with a stress-is-debilitating mindset, stress feels harder to deal with, performance and well-being are diminished, and the unhealthy effects of stress increase. Add to this, you are more likely to be stymied by even small and meaningless stressors, overreacting to them and perceiving them as insurmountable obstacles, not to mention missing out on potentially powerful opportunities for learning, growth, or service. In the end, a stress-is-debilitating mindset becomes a self-fulfilling prophecy. Not because the situation is actually more stressful but because your beliefs can block you from the benefits that are available to you.

The same holds true the other way. The more you accept the full picture of stress and its enhancing potential, the less your instinct will be to react with fight-or-flight and the more naturally you can tap into your challenge-based stress responses. This in turn drives the enhancing effects of stress in a positively reinforcing cycle.

A final point of clarification. Enlisting a "yes, and" stress mindset does not replace the value and need for emotional regulation strategies such as mindfulness, exercise, and reframing practices. Instead, it makes them easier to draw on and amplifies their positive effects. Learning how to embrace a "yes, and" stress mindset is the next step, but before we go there...

Remember Sandy?

The influence of your mindset is not always evident, but it is always significant. Ask yourself: where might I be missing positive opportunities simply because I've already labeled a situation or person a problem? This was the question Sandy needed to answer.

In reflection, Sandy realized that before she even opened Tom's email, she'd decided it would be triggering because of the mindset she held about Tom. While their relationship was difficult, Sandy had to acknowledge that this wasn't a "Triggering Tom" issue, it was a mindset issue, and the mindset that needed to be changed was hers. *(I should know, because in this scenario, Sandy was actually me.)*

11

Transforming Your Stress Response

WHEN you read the words "old person," what is the first thing that comes to mind? In the United States, the number one answer is "memory loss." In China, it's "wisdom." Drawing on decades of research, Yale professor Becca Levy finds that how you answer this question can have a major impact on how you age, potentially adding as much as seven-and-a-half years to your life.

But an important clarification needs to be made: people don't age better or live longer simply because they think more positively. Instead, holding an age-positive mindset increases the likelihood people will engage in actions to make the belief true. This includes eating healthier, staying hydrated, exercising, socializing, seeing their doctor more regularly, right down to properly following medication instructions.

The same goes for a "yes, and" stress mindset. As humans, we have an internal desire to live in alignment with our beliefs. The "yes, and" stress mindset is enhancing because it makes you more prone to take the actions, including the willingness to do the hard, often uncomfortable, uncertain, sometimes unpopular, and usually inconvenient things to stay congruent with those beliefs and your desired outcomes. The key here is that it takes *intentional actions* to make that happen.

Feel, Reveal, and Deal
. . . .

The good news is that there is a three-step process to help you take the actions to embrace a "yes, and" stress mindset: feel, reveal, deal.

In summary, the process starts by first checking in with what you *feel* and naming the emotion to help push the processing to the prefrontal cortex. A "yes, and" stress mindset isn't about focusing exclusively on the positives; it is embracing *all* the possibilities of stress. As such, the next step is to use your emotional reactions to *reveal* the possibilities of connecting to a deeper sense of meaning and assess whether your reactions are contributing to what matters most to you. Finally, you *deal* with the stressor by clarifying your goals and taking actions that move you toward them.

Step #1: FEEL the Stress

The true power of a "yes, and" stress mindset is that it embraces all the possibilities of stress: the good and the bad, the hard and the helpful, the strengths it builds and the struggles it creates.

Emodiversity is a term coined by researchers studying the benefits of diverse emotions. One of those researchers, Anthony Ong from Cornell University, illustrates the value of emotional diversity by comparing our emotional health to an ecosystem. He explains that in a biodiverse ecosystem each species has its role and contributes to the overall health and robustness of the ecosystem. Any system becomes more vulnerable if a single species is overabundant or depleted. However, when each species is free to contribute its diverse value, the system becomes more resilient and adaptable overall.

So is the case with your emotions. All emotions, including fear, obligation, and guilt, play an important role in strengthening your internal emotional ecosystem. They provide valuable information, directing you to something that wants your attention.

Notice your emotions. While most strategies focus on tempering the feelings of stress as quickly as possible, the first step to approach stress with a "yes, and" stress mindset is the opposite. It starts by actually feeling the stress and checking in with yourself about the emotions you are experiencing.

Begin by noticing how emotions are showing up for you throughout your body, the thoughts being generated, the actions you are wanting or not wanting to take. This step will come more naturally the more you are integrating in KVI (Key Vitality Indicator) energy check-ins. Not only does having KVIs help you keep your finger on the pulse of your energy in general, but you will learn to recognize and distinguish emotions along with their associated physical sensations to better address your needs.

Just as with stress, there are no "good" and "bad" emotions; how you interpret and respond to them is what matters. Unfortunately, most of us have learned to ignore, resist, or fight with hard emotions. We are often afraid that if we acknowledge difficult emotions, we will get stuck in them and feel overwhelmed by them. Nevertheless, acknowledging what you are feeling is critical to moving through the emotion in the most beneficial way.

Shift processing from the amygdala to the prefrontal cortex. Research by Matthew Lieberman has shown that when you simply acknowledge and label the emotions you are feeling or the experience you are having, it shifts the processing of stress out of the automatic, reactive amygdala to the more conscious and deliberate prefrontal cortex. When responding from the prefrontal cortex, you can reflect on your motivations, goals, and values and take actions in congruence with them.

A few important notes here. First, by naming your feeling or the experience you're having, you are *not* trying to change it, find the opportunity in it, or control it in any way. Second, emotions pass. Your role is simply to notice and acknowledge what you are thinking and feeling. This takes practice and is one reason why mindfulness meditation can be so valuable. A goal of mindfulness is to change your relationship with your emotions so they do not affect you as negatively or intensely, not to rid yourself of emotions. With practice, you can improve your ability to simply notice emotions without getting hooked by them or judging yourself or the circumstances for their existence.

One strategy to avoid getting unnecessarily attached to your emotions is adding the words "I feel" before naming the emotion or your interpretation of the experience. This creates space between you and what you are experiencing to make things more manageable. After all, you aren't your emotions or your thoughts.

Check out how different this is: You were in a meeting, and you didn't explain your idea well. After the meeting, you think to yourself, "I suck" versus, "I feel like I sucked in the meeting today." One is a judgment of you as a person, and the other is an authentic assessment of what you felt about the experience. Or perhaps it is shifting your language from "I'm overwhelmed" to "I feel overwhelmed." The first makes the emotion a representation of you and the second separates you from your emotions.

As counterintuitive as it sounds, part of what it means to be good at stress is to increase your discomfort tolerance to those initial signals of stress that you often don't like. When you feel angry, anxious, or overwhelmed, the skill is getting better at feeling that discomfort and not freaking out, checking out, numbing out, or shaming yourself into positivity. Over time you can learn how to stay with the emotion in service of moving through it.

Step #2: Identify What Your Stress REVEALS

The second step to elicit a "yes, and" stress mindset is based on the fact that we feel stress when we perceive that something we care about is at stake. The first step was to allow your emotions to come to the surface; rather than getting swept away by them, the second step is to shift into examination mode.

Assess your emotions and reactions. Since your emotions are informational data, get curious about what they are communicating to you. Ask yourself, what is upsetting me in this situation and why do I care about it?

Now, without judgment, self-assess your current reactions. Perhaps the biggest benefit of acknowledging emotions you are feeling and why the situation matters to you is that it becomes easier to recognize when your reactions are positively contributing to or negatively working in opposition (and initially they often are) to what matters most to you.

Find the meaning. One of the most common questions I am asked about boosting one's Work Vitality Quotient is, "Can you increase your Work Vitality Quotient if you don't like, let alone love, your work?" Addressing this question requires two reminders: First, loving your work is *not* a pre-requisite for reclaiming your vitality. Second, feeling vital means you feel energized, capable, resourceful, and connected to a sense of meaning or purpose.

Instead of focusing on finding work you love (and being miserable where you currently are), to cultivate vitality, shift the question you ask yourself to: How do I find what I love in the work I do? In other words, find what is meaningful to you: what can you bring to your work or what impact do you want to have as a result of your work and on the people around you? Your answers will give you a pre-calibrated "meaning" compass to connect with, to align your resources with, and to guide your actions in a way that matters to you—even if you don't love the actual work.

This same approach can be used to embrace a "yes, and" stress mindset. To help, there are three perspectives that make it easier to connect to a sense of meaning and expand the possibilities present in a stress-filled situation. Reflect on the following questions. How can this be a chance to...

- **Grow yourself:** to bring your energy-enhancing strengths to what you do, to learn, develop, build awareness, test yourself, expand experiences, practice a skill, or face a fear?

- **Give to others:** to be of service, to be a role model, to contribute to the growth, the development, the support, the protection, or the needs of others or to a mission bigger than yourself?

- **Ground in values:** to demonstrate integrity, bravery, authenticity, determination, to act in alignment with values, beliefs, and principles, or ground your actions in joy, peace, gratitude, love, or appreciation?

While I firmly believe not everything has a bright side, I also believe that there is a possibility of connecting to a deeper sense of meaning even in our most difficult moments. This approach is vastly different than looking for the good in adversity. Instead, think of this as creating purposeful energy versus positive feelings.

Step #3: DEAL With the Stress to Move toward Your Goals

Your Work Vitality Quotient is increased when your energy is directed toward what matters to you—in a way that is healthy for you. The process of embracing a "yes, and" stress mindset shifts seeing stress as the heart of the problem, to a valuable part of the process and energizing you forward.

As such, the final step involves accepting reality so you can redirect your attention to what you can control, draw on your resources, and take action toward your goals in a healthy and productive way.

Stop fighting reality. Fully embracing a "yes, and" stress mindset requires accepting the reality of the situation causing you stress in order to effectively deal with it. Too often we expend tremendous volumes of energy and effort fighting reality based on what we wish were true, what we want to be different, and what we believe should happen. Instead, focus on the facts of reality in the moment. Acceptance doesn't mean you settle for things as they are, it means you start from what is actually happening when planning how to move forward. This approach provides the freedom to lean into the messiness, ambiguity, and nuance of the challenges you face.

Get clear on your goals. One of the mistakes people make is that they confuse *coping with stress*, which is often to lessen the negative impact, with *working with stress*. By connecting to the opportunity to create meaning in response to an undesirable stressful event, it then makes it easier to refocus on how to authentically approach the challenge and get clarity on outcomes that you'd like to achieve, which, among others, may include:

- A relationship you want to strengthen.

- A moment you want to feel present in.

- A change you want to make.

- A value you want to live by.

- A commitment you want to follow through on.

- A behavior you want to model.

Take actions toward what matters. Now is the time to ask yourself, what actions are within my control that will move me toward my goal? Remember, your stress response, whether challenge- or threat-driven, is designed to provide you the energy and resources to meet the demands of a situation and move you to action. The opportunity is recognizing that you have a diverse range of stress responses available and leveraging the best one to help you. Ask yourself, what other resources can I draw on to help me get there? And then get to work implementing them.

Feel, Reveal, Deal in Action
. . . .

Lewis was a director of human resources at a large PR firm. When his new boss, the chief human resource officer (CHRO), was named, Lewis's heart sank. This person had a reputation of surrounding himself with people who would tell him exactly what he wanted to hear. Although Lewis was part of senior management, he was not a part of the CHRO's inner circle. He was anxious about the direction the CHRO was taking and the potential impact the new strategy was having on his already-stretched-too-thin team. It turns out, he was not alone in his reservations. With increasing frequency, meetings centered on commiserating over the decisions the CHRO was making and Lewis often found himself joining in. As much as he enjoyed his actual work and his team, following a particularly frustrating week of meetings discussing the new strategy, Lewis was seriously contemplating if it was time to leave.

Let's look at how Lewis could work through this scenario with the three-step feel, reveal, deal process.

Step #1: Feel

Start with curiosity and check in with yourself by asking, what am I feeling right now?

Lewis was feeling unheard and unincluded by his new boss. He felt like he was letting his team down by not being able to influence the CHRO's decisions or overarching strategy. He felt betrayed that his colleagues with the ear of the CHRO were just going along with it. Personally, Lewis also realized that his commitment to work had become consuming and it was taking a toll on him. He felt out of shape, tired, and increasingly impatient, judgmental, and angry.

Step #2: Reveal

Shift to examination mode and ask yourself, why does this situation matter to me? (After all, you don't feel stress about things you don't care about.) Honestly self-assess, what are my current reactions and are they contributing to what matters to me? Finally, how can I see

Increasing your
Work Vitality Quotient
isn't accomplished
in the pursuit of a life
without stress; it's
found in a life full of
things that matter.

---

this as an opportunity to expand the possibilities and connect to something meaningful?

The reason he was struggling was because many of the things that Lewis cared most about felt at stake. What Lewis personally valued was approaching things with realistic optimism, demonstrating empathy, and being a role model. For teamwork and collaboration, he cared about working professionally and in alignment with his values, and protecting his team from burnout. Broadly, he cared about helping to shed the negative stigma people had toward HR, creating influential programs to be seen as a partner, and truly helping people within the organization.

Lewis's current reactions to this point were to vent, shut down in meetings, and send frustrated, curt emails, which only served to establish his position as an adversary in the eyes of the CHRO, pushing him further outside the circle of influence. He was also inadvertently deepening the us-versus-them dynamic that was growing within the HR division and across the firm by commiserating in meetings and criticizing the company. He was taking on extra work in an attempt to lighten the load on his team, which not only kept him from the more strategic work he was responsible for, but also the extra workload on top of an already heavy one was exhausting him. He was resentfully checking email late into the night and working on weekends, which were not the behaviors that he wanted to role model. While he was worried about his team burning out, his actions were burning him out. Doing this reality check made it clear to him that his reactions were not helping and they definitely were not in alignment with any of his values.

Shifting to a mindset of meaning, Lewis was energized by collaboration and finding solutions to complex problems. He recognized that this situation was an opportunity to do both while also grounding himself in his values and empowering his team to grow and be a part of the solution. Lastly, on a personal level, he realized this was a meaningful chance for him to grow as a leader. While he didn't need to agree with the CHRO's decisions, as a leader his job was to clear and guide the way forward in a positive and productive way. Where Lewis initially felt stuck and angry, he now appreciated the possibilities available.

Step #3: Deal

Move into action by getting clear on your goals, accepting the reality of the situation, and then asking yourself: what actions are within my control that will help me move toward my goals in a positive and healthy way?

Lewis had to accept that currently the CHRO had a different vision and fighting that reality and his boss wasn't helping. In fact, it actually meant he was losing any opportunity to influence things and provide a point of view Lewis felt the CHRO was missing. Shifting to acceptance meant Lewis could redirect his attention to his relationship with his boss, use his energy to better understand the strategy, and challenge himself and his team to refocus on how the new strategy (or at least parts of it) could work instead of why it wouldn't.

He assessed his repertoire of stress responses. Reaching out and connecting with others, as well as finding the opportunity in a complex situation, were two challenge responses that motivated him. Propelled by this deeper sense of meaning, he used this energy to pull his team together to strategize. Aligning to his values of optimism and empathy, he challenged himself and his team to put themselves in the new CHRO's shoes. From this vantage point it was easier to appreciate that naturally, the CHRO surrounded himself with people that supported him and whom he viewed as helpful in putting his strategy in place. Focusing on what was controllable, Lewis and his team brainstormed how to best implement the strategic plan and what resources would amplify its success. They developed a sound and unbiased business proposal to take to the CHRO to secure the needed resources. He and the team then stepped back to look at how they—on a team level—could implement the new strategy in the healthiest ways possible. Together they clarified communication expectations, availability boundaries, and established weekly team check-ins to connect and assess how to best use resources and support one another.

Completing the Stress Cycle
....

Stress itself is not bad or unhealthy. However, one major contributor to the unhealthy effects of stress is an inability to get a break from it to recover. While feel, reveal, deal helps you to embrace a "yes, and" stress mindset, when it comes to working well with stress, there is actually a fourth step needed to complete the stress cycle in a healthy way. This step serves to further amplify the effect of the "yes, and" stress mindset. The fourth step is to *heal*—to create space between you and stress so you can redirect your efforts to recover, replenish, and reinvigorate your energy. After all, vitality is generated by both using your energy in the pursuit of meaningful things and refueling it in deliberate and skillful ways. In the final section of the book, you will do a deep dive into how to best heal and re-energize.

For Lewis, one way this fourth step of healing was accomplished was by joining a dragon boat racing team. Meeting new people, getting outside and on the water which always calmed him, having an after-work commitment that forced him to put an end to his workday, as well as putting himself in rookie-mode (as he was the newest member to dragon boating) turned out to be game changing. Not only did joining the dragon boat team help provide some new perspectives for the pressure his boss may have felt as the newest member of the executive team, but more importantly, it helped Lewis to feel more restored. While work was still very stressful, by expanding his focus from just work, he ended up feeling reconnected to the aspects of it that he found most rewarding while also engaging in a life that fulfilled him.

Embracing a "yes, and" stress mindset is by no means a cure-all. Nor does it mean you'll avoid fight-or-flight reactions or the potentially negative effects of stress. However, it will help guide you toward what you want and boost your Work Vitality Quotient by making you feel more purposeful, resourceful, and energized in the face of stress. Most importantly, being intentional with your mindset helps you work with stress in a way that makes you stronger in the long run.

Human beings are complex and stress is as well. At any given moment, opposing things can be true. Stress can feel incredibly hard, and it can be helpful. Yes, this makes solutions less clear, but if you are willing to accept that complexity brings opportunity, embracing the paradoxes of stress can be freeing. The road to increasing your Work Vitality Quotient isn't to pursue a life without stress; it's found in a life full of things that matter.

12

Keeping Small Stress Small

I LOVE the TV show *Naked and Afraid*. It is an American reality series that follows two people who have never met who are tasked with surviving the wilderness together for twenty-one days. The fact that people are naked (although appropriately blurred for TV) may seem like clickbait to entice people to watch, and yes that does set it apart from other shows, but the goal is to create a real "survivalist" experience. The participants must survive with nothing more than a single item of their choosing to help them forage in their environment. The locations range from deserts to rain forests.

Watching from the warm comforts of my home, I am drawn to observing these people navigate the mental aspect of survival. The entire experience is a giant stress experiment. Apart from being attacked by any number of predators, the biggest stressors include the need to build shelter, find water and food, sleep in the elements, not to mention create and maintain fire. Understandably, people often quit before completing the full twenty-one-day challenge.

Yet, with all the struggles and dangers, there is one thing that can break even the most experienced survivalist: mosquitoes (or any small, stinging, biting insect). The constant assault of stings on the participants' bodies, all day and all night, simply wears them down. Sure, building shelter and fire, finding food, and fighting off predators is energy-taxing and stressful—but working on them *feels* meaningful. When stress feels meaningful, people are more likely to persevere in the face of discomfort and adversity. But add the constant buzzing and stinging of mosquitoes and it's a different story. The insects are irritating, there is no way to get rid of them, and they make everything harder and less enjoyable.

Life's Mosquitoes
. . . .

The impact of mosquitoes is a helpful analogy for how we experience small, often predictable everyday stressors, including traffic jams, juggling family schedules, coordinating home repairs, or arguing with your kids about how long they can play video games. At work it might be triggering emails, inefficient meetings, unclear expectations, unreliable colleagues, and seemingly needless bureaucracy. To be clear, none of these ever *feels* small in the moment. Yet on the grand scale of things, they aren't life altering. Unfortunately, it doesn't change the fact that they are still frustrating and energy consuming.

Like the sting of a mosquito, daily hassles are irritating but each alone is manageable. It's when the next three stings come before you've even been able to swat away the first that the accumulation of small stressors begins to have an oversized effect. Feeling overwhelmed by the small stressors in turn exacerbates the impact of the big stressors, until you feel totally stressed out.

As we've seen through the journey of rethinking stress and its impact on our Work Vitality Quotient, often how we carry the load of stress has a bigger impact than the load of stress itself. A 2014 study by Carolyn Aldwin investigating the effects of long-term stress on mortality followed a group of men between 1989 and 2010. It examined how stress, including significant life events and smaller everyday stressors, influenced mortality rates. Interestingly, men who felt they experienced more daily hassles, whether real or just perceived, were three times more likely to die within the study period than those who approached daily hassles as a part of life.

The Stress Spiral

While conducting interviews for the research of this book I asked people to track what activities or experiences gave them a boosted sense of vitality. Without fail, taking on meaningful challenges such as pursuing bold goals, fostering important relationships, and living a full life were all boosters. The biggest drainers? You guessed it, the small, daily mosquito-like frustrations that feel like meaningless obstacles to all the big stuff that does matter.

Imagine you're finalizing a complex proposal for a client that, if selected, would mean you hit your targets for the quarter—a significant but meaningful source of stress. The meaningless mosquito stressors are the ping-pong of unhelpful and curt emails traded with finance as they pressure you to add next year's price increases to a budget you've already negotiated with the client... add to that your kids fighting over the iPad in the next room... add to that you still haven't picked up food for the barbeque tomorrow... add to that the toilet squeals so loudly every time it's flushed you're sure a pipe is going to explode... and it will probably happen during the barbeque!

Small, meaningless daily frustrations drain our time and energy, and they leave us annoyed long after the stress has passed. Over time, unless we actively reset our perspective, it gets harder to see these frustrations as something that everyone experiences; instead, they start feeling like one big burden that we're uniquely forced to deal with, keeping us from the happiness and success we're supposed to have.

Remember the research on daily stress and mortality? In a media release, Aldwin summed it up perfectly: "It's not the number of hassles that does you in, it's the perception of them being a big deal

When stress
feels meaningful,
people are
more likely to
persevere.

that causes problems." Intercepting the stress spiral early is the key to keeping small stress small.

Head Strategies
. . . .

There are three things that affect the impact of stress on your health and your Work Vitality Quotient as a whole: if you get a break from stress, what you believe about the nature of stress, and how you respond in the face of stress. When it comes to small stressors that feel meaningless and that you often can't control or just separate yourself from, how you respond to them is the biggest factor in the impact they will have on you. The good news is that's also the part you have the most control over. Studying people who have higher self-reported levels of vitality, I kept waiting to hear about huge cataclysmic changes that altered their lives and helped them deal with stress. Instead, what I heard about was tiny, daily perspective shifts.

I have distilled four of the most powerful and easily accessible perspective shifts:

- Jump to...

- Decide to...

- Add to...

- Get to...

These four simple wonder-based perspective shifts help you act on what you can control: you and your responses. These are what I call "head strategies" because they focus on choosing your perspective. When we start talking about energy management in the final section, we'll expand on these by incorporating strategies that involve your body, your breath, and breaks.

Jump To...

The first perspective shift is mentally jumping to "future you" or "past you." We all have days when we're tired, less productive, and less focused. In response, the further we get into our day, the more anxious we feel about everything we haven't done. People who have a higher Work Vitality Quotient tend to recognize when they are struggling; instead of beating themselves up for it or trying to work themselves out of it, they shift their focus to what they can do to help their future self feel more rested, energized, focused, and productive. The reality is no one is productive every day. When you face a hard day, start with self-compassion, and ask yourself, what is the kindest, most helpful thing I can do for myself right now to make tomorrow a better day?

Alternatively, instead of mentally jumping forward, you can jump back to past you. Start by asking yourself, when has *past me* experienced a moment like this? What wisdom from previous experiences can I draw on to help me in this situation?

A quick exercise I find helpful is to write a *resilience résumé*. Just as a job résumé showcases your skills and positive attributes, a resilience résumé lists experiences that you got through and made you more resourceful. The action of writing it out reinforces how strong, adaptable, brave, and resilient you are. Keep it close, update it often, and the next time you feel as if life is running you over, pull it out. If there is one thing for sure, more challenges and change will come. Your resilience résumé is proof positive that you can handle whatever happens and serves as a reminder of all that you've already done.

Decide To...

Let it go. This perspective shift acknowledges that not everything needs to be a battle, nor does everything deserve the same level of time, energy, and attention. Letting go isn't about suppressing your emotions or trying to make yourself not care, it's about deciding to let your emotional connection in the moment, go. If not forever, at least for the moment.

To authentically learn to let go, it helps to work with the design of the brain. Remember, to shift emotions from being processed primarily by the amygdala, you can activate the wonder circuitry of your prefrontal cortex by prompting self-reflective questions. Try this simple "7x7" practice. The next time you face a daily hassle or have a frustrating interaction, ask yourself the following "7x7" time-allotment questions:

- Will this frustration matter seven years from now?

- What about seven months from now?

- What about seven weeks, seven days, seven hours, seven minutes, or seven seconds from now?

Think about how many things happen in a day that will not matter by the end of the day, let alone seven minutes later. Yet we blow things out of proportion by reacting as if they will matter seven years from now! Does this exercise change the situation that annoyed you? No, but it helps you be intentional about how much time and energy you will give to something and how much mental real estate you want to rent out to that frustration.

Another way of letting go involves letting go of the level of expectation you have for yourself. Before presenting to a financial organization, I spoke with the CEO and I asked him if there was any specific message he wanted his people to take away. His surprising answer was: "I wish they realized that there are very few times that we need to be perfect. Most of the time, good enough really is good enough." The perfectionist reading this just bristled, I'm sure. I suspect you've seen the quote "good is the enemy of great," but, just as dangerously, great can be the enemy of good enough.

While some days your best does require giving 100 percent effort, on other days, the healthiest and most helpful, vitality-generating thing you can do is to be good enough, let it go, and move on. The decision to relinquish perfection, overinvestment, and the rigid expectations you have set for yourself instantly allows you to maneuver and adapt to the world with a greater range of motion and freedom. Sometimes that *is* the most invigorating perspective you can take.

Add To...

We all have things we don't enjoy doing but that are responsibilities, sometimes known as "adulting." This perspective shift is about integrating something that gives you joy or adds more fun to something that otherwise is undesirable. I call this "funtegration."

Fun + integration = funtegration

Stuck in traffic? Try listening to a fiction book by a favorite author. Love '80s classic rock ballads? Make a playlist with your favorites to listen to while cutting the grass. I truly do not enjoy folding and putting laundry away or doing my weekly meal prepping. However, I have a favorite British series that I watch only while doing these two things. I don't watch it any other time. That way, even though I dislike folding laundry, I can look forward to watching the series.

Sometimes it's impossible or undesirable to integrate additional activities into a task. In those cases you can add in fun and joy in a less direct way. A 2016 study asked university staff members and students to record a short-term goal they were striving to accomplish. Over the following week, they tracked the minor annoyances as well as simple pleasures experienced throughout the day. As expected, on days filled with hassles but few pleasures, goal progress was hindered. However, on days where daily hassles were prevalent but participants recorded more simple pleasures, such as a nice interaction with a barista, hearing their favorite song, or laughing with a coworker, they made more progress toward their goals.

While nothing was done to reduce or remove daily stress, simply looking for and noticing pleasurable things helped buffer the effects

What is the
kindest thing you can
do for yourself right
now to make tomorrow
a better day?

_____

of stress and inched people closer to their goals. Studies have found that when asking people to track moments of joy or gratitude or appreciation over a period of time, the volume of *perceived* positive experiences increases—not necessarily because people experienced more of them, but because their brains were primed to look for good things and add them to their overall experience.

Get To...

The final perspective shift is moving from a mindset of "I have to" to a one of "I get to." Three years after being diagnosed, my mother died of an aggressive breast cancer. In the first year and a half following her initial diagnosis she underwent surgery, hormone therapy, as well as chemotherapy and radiation. As tough as it was, it was worth it as her cancer went into a full remission. In celebration, we planned a Caribbean vacation. A few weeks before the trip, she sent me a text: "I get to go bathing suit shopping!"

For most of us, especially those over the age of twenty-five, bathing suit shopping is rarely seen as a treat. Bad lighting, multi-angled mirrors, standing in your underwear with only a curtain separating you and everyone else is not most people's idea of a great time. In addition to this general unpleasantness, my mom also had severe psoriasis, a skin condition resulting in red, scaly patches of skin. Never one to do anything in moderation, she had an aggressive form and it covered 80 percent, sometimes more, of her legs. As you can imagine, I had never heard my mom excited about anything that revealed too much of her skin—until that day.

Pre-cancer, my mom viewed bathing suit shopping as something to dread, hating her skin. Following her remission, she viewed it as something she got to do despite her skin. The psoriasis didn't change, her perspective did. I am so glad because as a result that vacation was filled with love and laughter—and provided me with lasting gratitude.

Sadly, my mother's cancer returned a few months after we got back. That was her last vacation. I believe anytime we experience a loss, whether it be the loss of a loved one or the loss of what we labeled as normal life, we can—if we choose to look for it—gain a deeper sense of appreciation, especially for the small things.

The final week of my mother's life was spent in a beautiful hospice. One of the center's traditions was to give family and friends the opportunity to record thoughts, feelings, drawings, or anything else that helped process the difficult emotions of saying goodbye to someone in a communal scrapbook. The book was always left in the shared common area. Sometimes I'd write in it and other times I just read through the entries left by others. I recall being struck by how often people reflected on the mundane moments. The same ones we often look at as daily hassles.

One entry read, "I'll miss talking to you when you make my lunch for school." I'm confident that whoever was making those lunches day after day—dealing with the complaints about what was being prepared, rushing to get people out the door, matching the right flavor of juice box with the right kid—would never have thought that those moments would be missed. I would also guess that whoever "had to" make those lunches would have made a million more, hassles and all, if they "got to" have just one more of those conversations with whomever wrote that entry.

You don't need to wait for those moments. Something remarkable happens when you are intentional about how you look at your life. This is how you ensure the small things don't keep you from the important things that truly matter.

PART
FOUR

Dear Energy,

how do I get more of you?

13

Re-energizing You

I REMEMBER it perfectly. I was sitting on the edge of the dock, looking out at the water and thinking it looked like floating diamonds, the way it glistened. My muscles were tired, but in that good way after you've physically challenged yourself. I had just closed my eyes and tipped my head back to get the full warmth of the sun on my face when it suddenly felt like a clamp tightened around my chest, squeezing out my breath. An internal heat radiated up my neck and face. A sense of panic ripped through my body, warning me that something was wrong. That was the onset of my first, and to date only, anxiety attack.

It occurred in the summer of 2009. I was working in sales, managing an intense and competitive market, which was precisely what I loved about it. Three years earlier, I had convinced the hiring manager that I could outwork anyone, so whatever I lacked in experience and expertise, I would make up for in sweat equity. And I did. I worked hard to know my products technically and invested my time and energy into building strong, trusting relationships. And it worked, at least for a while. My all-in work ethic resulted in winning top awards and career opportunities.

Three years into the role, though, the energy, enthusiasm, and drive for the work that I'd once genuinely enjoyed felt elusive. I perpetually felt behind in work and life and as a result, fun and relaxation felt like a reward that I never deserved. Any downtime became catch-up time to the point where I felt anxious when my husband and I received an invite to a weekend event because going would mean I'd have less time to work.

I wasn't just overwhelmed; I was tired all the time. I had chronic pain in my neck that resulted in a constant headache. I couldn't remember when it started or when having a headache just became the status quo, but I did have enough sense to recognize that I needed a break.

That's how I ended up in Germany, taking a two-week-long professional development course on my "vacation." When I first investigated the course and noticed the location, I thought, "Perfect! I can get in a bit of time off, learn to fix whatever I am doing wrong, find my spark, and get myself back on top." I booked my flight, blocked my calendar, packed my bags, and was off.

One notable caveat to this story, while this course was held in Germany, I did not speak German. Luckily, it was being delivered in English, but my lack of German still posed a significant problem that became evident upon my arrival. At that time, hotel internet connections were not as accessible as they are today, which meant if I were going to keep an eye on work email, I would need to use the hotel lobby computer. Seeing as everything was in German, that was not an easy option. Feeling partly panicked and partly relieved that accessing work would be difficult, I decided to just disconnect from work email while there.

The hotel was directly on the water and had kayaks available for guest use. To distract me from the worry of not being in contact with work, I started a ritual of waking up, heading down to the water, and going for a morning kayak before breakfast.

It was on the eighth or ninth morning, while I was taking in the beauty of the day, when I was gripped by that anxiety attack.

I can recall it so vividly because of the paradoxical experience—the environment around me was so beautiful and serene. Yet, internally, it felt like a chaotic storm closing in on me. My mind raced, looking for the answer to what was wrong, and in response, I did the only thing I could think to do: I focused on slowing down my breath. As someone managing a chronic autoimmune condition for the last two decades, I had learned to tune in to and address what was happening in my body. And then I got my answer to what was wrong—nothing—nothing was wrong in that moment.

The normal headache I'd had for the past three years was gone. The constant tiredness was replaced with energy. Instead of feeling distracted, frustrated, and stressed, I felt grounded, enthusiastic, and rested. This was the complete opposite experience of what I had become accustomed to. The distinction between the two states at that moment was so dramatic that my nervous system reacted as if I were in danger, spurring an anxiety attack.

I've never forgotten my experience that day on the dock in Germany or the indelible impact it had on me. Partly because it made me realize how much I'd lowered the bar on my physical, mental, and emotional health, but also the toll running on fumes for so long had taken. But mostly because I felt like I'd found myself again, which was scary because, until that moment, I hadn't even realized I'd lost myself.

It's Not about Stepping Back, Slowing Down, and Restricting More

It's tempting to read about my experience on the dock and assume that raising your Work Vitality Quotient requires—or is even dependent on—taking vacations, but that is an oversimplification. Or perhaps now that you've explored the success traps and your approach to stress, you are expecting that I'll tell you that you need to pull back and rest more. It would make sense, as self-care and rest advice often skews toward doing less and restricting more. While sometimes those messages are warranted, and those actions are needed, the less-is-best perspective leads us to believe that slowing down, stepping back, and eliminating things is the best way to fill our energy tank back up.

The challenge is that when it comes to raising your Work Vitality Quotient, at best, this view is far too narrow. As we've seen in high-stress work environments, intensified by on-demand expectations, all-or-nothing thinking sets in, making the advice to ease up appear either impossible due to circumstances or undesirable if it means sacrificing success or going against our values.

At worst, the narrow focus on slowing down leads you to mistakenly disconnect from the people, practices, and pursuits that infuse you with vitality in the first place.

Expanding Your View of Self-Care

Following one of my keynotes, a woman named Helen from the audience shared that she'd recently taken on a new role. As exciting as it was, the new role also came with a longer commute, leaving her exhausted when she got home at night. As a result, she found herself increasingly less patient with her two young kids and with little time left for her spouse. When she talked this over with family and friends, their advice was predictable: do less.

Acting on the advice, she began eliminating many of her discretionary after-work commitments, one of which was attending meetings for a professional association. Over the coming months, Helen found that without the commitments, she did have more time in the evenings. Unfortunately, she didn't find herself more patient with the kids, nor did she feel any more energized. Instead, she now felt a new sense of emptiness.

Following our conversation, Helen realized that attending her industry association events actually was a self-care practice, as it provided the opportunity to connect with others, as well as reflect and learn new skills, personally and professionally. While there was an up-front time, energy, and effort commitment, each were repaid tenfold by the vitality infusion she got from her involvement.

Helen's story is a perfect example of why a more expanded approach to self-care is needed. Instead of thinking about it as stepping back, slowing down, and eliminating things, think of self-care as the act of *changing direction and re-engaging in other parts of your life* that nourish, refuel, and reinvigorate your vitality.

Sometimes this will include powering down, staying still, turning inwards, and creating space for solitude. Other times this will mean powering up, connecting with others, pushing yourself out of your comfort zone to learn something new, and accelerating in a different direction.

Self-Care Misconceptions

It can be tricky separating what's trendy from what's true, but these days most people recognize self-care as a mainstream concept in the conversations about well-being. We are finally starting to talk about our mental and emotional health with the same urgency as we've talked about our physical health. The discussions about well-being have also penetrated the walls of our workplaces. An ever-growing body of research builds a compelling case that self-care-driven practices are not a separate entity supporting high performance; they are an essential element of high performance.

Still, there is something to the language we use and the meaning we attribute to the concept of self-care that can cause resistance. Let's clear a few things up.

It's Not a Bubble Bath

The term "self-care" has become a consumerist buzzword with advertisers often associating it with privileged people (particularly women) pampering themselves with spa treatments. But this is a limited and exclusionary view.

Think about
self-care as *changing
direction and
re-engaging in other
parts of life.*

Self-care includes rituals, practices, or experiences that you engage in to support caring for your vitality, including your health, well-being, and performance. There is no one-size-fits-all formula. It covers a diverse range of things that can be a spa treatment but also includes staying hydrated, setting boundaries, practicing gratitude, volunteering your time, sitting around a bonfire with neighbors telling stories and laughing late into the night, or finding a quiet corner to do a two-minute meditation while you take a few cleansing breaths. You do not have to spend money to practice self-care; after all, breathing doesn't cost you anything!

It's Not Selfish

Turning your attention toward yourself can *feel* selfish if it feels like you are taking time, energy, and attention away from others who truly appreciate it, who certainly want it, and who sometimes may genuinely need it. This is especially true for people whose values and identity are connected to helping and selflessly being of service, regardless of the ask. To clarify, self-care is not selfish, but it's not necessarily a simple or easy choice either.

Throughout the pandemic, I was honored to have the opportunity to work with frontline healthcare workers, emergency response coordinators, and hospital administrators. I saw firsthand how challenging it was for them to shift their time, energy, and attention toward caring for themselves when they had patients and people, including their teammates, depending on them. I also saw and continue to see the burnout that results when self-care falls to the bottom (or right off) of the list of priorities. You can't give what you don't have. Instead of viewing self-care as a selfish act, choose to recognize it as the conduit that allows you to think clearly, act generously, and have the resources to genuinely be of service to others.

It's Not Self-Indulgent

On the flip side, self-care can feel self-indulgent, especially when it's prioritized preventively to maintain or boost our health and well-being.

I once sent an end-of-day meeting invite to a colleague who immediately called to apologize. They then when on to explain that after learning they had high blood pressure had started working with a personal trainer after work and the meeting request overlapped with that training time.

Whether externally or internally generated, fear, guilt, and obligation can make you feel as if you need to justify or defend why you're doing something for yourself. Why you're going on vacation when work is busy (because let's be honest, it's always busy). Or why you're choosing to do something fun, personally important, or doing nothing at all in the evening instead of answering email or accepting a meeting. You don't have to have an excuse, be busy, or be in desperate need of a break to feel justified in taking one. Instead, see self-care as your commitment to playing the long game of bolstering your Work Vitality Quotient.

It's Not a Reward

For the to-do list makers reading this, rest is not a reward for completing everything on your to-do list. It is a right independent of achievements, productivity, or how warranted it feels.

Have you ever said, "Once I get the garage organized, I will reward myself by brushing my teeth"? I am reasonably confident the answer to that is "No!" You don't think of brushing your teeth as a right you earn, do you? It is a way you care for yourself. So consider this: you also don't need to earn the right to hang out with your pet, go to a basketball game with friends, or get a full night's sleep.

Rest should not be reserved for the moment everything and everyone else have been taken care of. You are a human and taking care of your well-being is a non-negotiable necessity to live and work in healthy, sustainable, and fulfilling ways. Understanding how to do that and doing it well is a skill this book will help you build, but giving yourself permission to do it—that is a choice *you* need to make.

Self-Care 2.0
. . . .

Social scientists have amassed a huge trove of compelling evidence pointing to the importance of self-care practices. The challenge is that with the range of options, choosing which practices will have the best vitality-boosting outcomes can feel daunting, especially when you are already feeling overwhelmed and exhausted.

My goal when researching how to best nourish, refuel, and reignite vitality was to identify the practices that, regardless of the type of day you are having, don't need to be big time consumers. Practices that are within your control to do and mostly independent of the involvement of others. And practices that are both accessible and sustainable over time.

The result of this research is an expanded view of self-care. Think of it as self-care 2.0. It is composed of a set of distinct categories of activities I call the "CARE Index." CARE includes:

- Connection

- Activation

- Restoration

- Exploration

If immediately you feel a prickling of panic at the idea of having more to do, rest assured you don't have to do all the CARE practices every day, all at once, or to the same degree. However, each practice is important in cultivating a robust and enduring Work Vitality Quotient.

I saw the impact of using the CARE Index in my work well before the pandemic, but following its onset, the structure it provided became even more evident. Over and over, I'd hear the same thing from family, friends, clients, and audiences, "I just can't seem to find that same motivation." Or, "I've always worked remotely, but I feel more stressed." Or, as I'm sure everyone reading this book has said at some point, "I feel like every day is melding into the next." Many people described feeling less focused, productive, and creative. These feelings were so widespread that Wharton professor and *New York Times*-bestselling author Adam Grant wrote an article about the feeling of "pandemic blah," or languishing. Languishing is the emotion of feeling stuck—not burned out and depressed, but not flourishing either. "Blah" also describes the feeling of a vitality deficit, which is a potential consequence when you neglect one or more of the CARE categories for too long.

Our brains, bodies, and souls need different inputs. We already know that people who demonstrate higher resilience levels also experience higher levels of emotional diversity. We know that regularly challenged brains are more robust, flexible, and adaptable. That is part of the power of the CARE Index; it fills gaps and expands experiences. If you're feeling alone and purposeless, focusing on *connection* in your community may create a sense of meaning. If you feel mentally exhausted from sitting in front of your computer for hours at a time, *activation* can help to release the energy locked up within you. If work is chaotic, *restoration* practices can bring a sense of peace. If you're feeling bored with a long-haul work project, *exploration* outside of work may reignite your inspiration.

In truth, many of us have never been taught how to decipher, manage, and replenish our energy. Personally, many of the activities that were re-energizing for me while in Germany were the same things I sacrificed at home. Either because I believed I didn't have enough time, didn't think they produced a "productive" enough outcome, or because I thought the activities got in the way of my professional goals. But most of all, I had too narrow a view of self-care and thought rest was about slowing down. While there was time to relax, overall slowing down was not how you'd describe my trip. What I didn't know then was the reason my time in Germany was so impactful was because of the incorporation of each of the CARE elements.

Your Path Back to You
. . . .

As you move through these final chapters, I hope it will be clear why I have chosen to focus on re-energizing you with CARE as the last step. Not because it is the least important element or that it comes after everything else has been taken care of. I have placed it at the end because addressing your energy to raise your Work Vitality Quotient is more than something you need to do—it is a skill you need to build. This requires coming to terms with your relationship to work as well as your beliefs about success, stress, and rest so you can shift them from obstacles keeping you from doing what you know is best, to working with the science of your brain and turning them into opportunities to do what's best.

While it takes some up-front work, the CARE Index will re-energize you so you can face the day with more openness, curiosity, and enthusiasm. It will help you pour your best into the world while ensuring you have the skills and structure to manage and protect your vitality, so you can do it all over again the next day.

You are a multifaceted person with a multifaceted life. Depending on your current roles and responsibilities, as well as your goals and interests, where you prioritize putting your energy and how you best replenish and reinvigorate that energy will differ. Remember, vitality is personal, so don't compare yourself to others. It is intentional, so you have to be willing to try things. It's dynamic, so some practices will be easy and will have an immediate positive and energizing impact, while others will require making hard and less enjoyable choices in the moment to invest in filling your vitality reservoir for the future.

If you feel as I did on that dock in Germany, someone who has lost a little bit of you, integrating the elements of CARE into your life is a surefire way to clear a path back to you. Not only that, I suspect you will discover parts of yourself that you didn't even know were lying dormant, just waiting to be revealed. That is the power of a vitality-fueled life.

14

The CARE Index

"IT WON'T hurt at all and is totally safe. All you need to do is lie still on the plastic surface. I'll push this button to activate the nails. They will rise simultaneously through all those tiny holes in the plastic, lifting you so you will be lying atop a bed of nails."

"Are you kidding?" my ten-year-old self thought.

When I was a child, one of my favorite things was to go to the science center. It was magical for a nerdy kid like me who loved figuring out how people and things worked. But when we got to the bed-of-nails exhibit, my intrigue turned to terror.

I was frozen with fear, but my little sister pushed past me to lie down on the table. Barely holding back tears, I was sure nails would pierce through her body. And then suddenly, there she was, lying on a bed of nails. "It's like magic," I said to the exhibit guide. And I'm sure I've exaggerated this moment in my head, but I swear I remember her saying with a wink, "It's not magic; it's science."

The physics behind the bed of nails is simple. Pressure equals force divided by area. To keep the nails from puncturing through whatever's on top of them, you either decrease the force pushing down on the nails or increase the surface area the pressure is dispersed across. This is why so many nails are placed tightly together—to disperse a person's weight evenly over a large surface area. This is also the physics of vitality.

When it comes to the pressure you feel from work and life, you can think of the demands you face as the force pushing down on you and your capacity to deal with those demands as your potential surface area. To lessen the effects of the demands you can either remove some, which unfortunately is not always possible. Or you can strengthen and broaden your capacity to handle them, which is within your control. The CARE Index is a science-backed framework to build and broaden your capacity to take on all of life's demands in pursuing bold goals, deep bonds, and big energy.

How to Use the CARE Index

We're going to look at each category of CARE—connection, activation, restoration, and exploration—in depth. As you review each category, note which ones you are naturally drawn toward. What are your go-to's, and which are the first to fall off when you are busy and tired?

A simple and powerful way to integrate the CARE Index is to grab a pen and paper and as you read through each category, record a list of potential activities you could do for each. To get a good diversity of answers, brainstorm with friends, family, and colleagues. We're going to return to this list, so keep it close by and have fun adding to it.

Connection

I was flying out of the Chicago airport heading home after a week of delivering five keynotes in different cities. Whereas I'd usually be exhausted by the time I caught my flight home, this flight was different. After my keynote, instead of hopping in the car and heading to the airport, I had lunch with work friends whose company I thoroughly enjoyed. Over the span of an hour and a half, we hugged, laughed, told stories, and shared our challenges, all while feasting on delicious fish and chips.

On the plane, I reflected on a funny exchange between my group and the restaurant's server. Chuckling to myself, I felt a flood of gratitude and a surge of aliveness pulse through my veins. The visit was over, but the energizing effect lingered. That is the power of connection. While it nourishes and replenishes energy, it also exponentially amplifies the vitality available to us, both in the moment and with a potent, lasting lag effect.

In the CARE Index, connection encompasses personal and professional relationships, as well as broader community connections, including feeling a sense of spiritual connection to something larger than ourselves. And while social media connections may not be the best representation of friendship, when the interactions are supportive and positive, being a part of online groups can create a powerful feeling of community. And of course, we can't overlook the deep sense of connection experienced through the unconditional love of our furry friends.

While most of our time, energy, and effort goes into strengthening our close-knit relationships (known as our "strong ties"), those frequent interactions, it turns out, aren't enough to truly fulfill our need for connection. Studies find that our informal and often spontaneous in-person interactions with acquaintances and even strangers (known as our "weak ties") are just as important. These weak-tie interactions, including seeing familiar faces at the neighborhood dog park, a colleague from a different department in the elevator, or a shared smile as you pass by a stranger on the street, are critical to creating a broader sense of belonging and connection to our communities, our places of work, and society at large.

If you spend significant time working from home, an important aspect in boosting your Work Vitality Quotient may be to intentionally leave the house and engage with the world through both your strong and weak ties to ensure your need for connection is fulfilled. In fact, just about every empirically validated study on physical and psychological well-being denotes connection as one of the most significant contributors. Positive relationships in which you feel accepted, valued, and cared for mitigate the potentially negative effects of stress and lower the risks of depression, anxiety, neurological illness, diabetes, heart attacks, and inflammatory diseases.

And it turns out, the vitality-boosting experience you get from relationships isn't just based on what you receive. Giving back to others, whether that be formally volunteering or informally being of service, is one of the most vitality-enhancing tools you have at your disposal.

Whether you are an introvert or extrovert, the replenishing effect of connection is especially heightened when you are mentally and emotionally engaged in the same experience with others. This is why when you enjoy something, whether a beautiful sunset, a delicious dessert, or a funny video, you are drawn to want to share it with others, which as it turns out, makes a good experience feel even better.

Simply put, your wellness is strongly dependent on your experience of "we-ness." With levels of loneliness on the rise, it is essential that we as a society build communities and workplaces and intentionally engage in activities that encourage connection. Relationships make us feel loved, allow us to show love, connect us to our shared humanity, bolster us through hardships, and serve as joy conduits. Most of all, connection is a fundamental human need critical to our most vital selves.

Activation

Activation is the second category in the CARE Index. What is clear from the science of movement is that exercise stimulates neurochemical and physiological changes that don't occur when you are sedentary. While there is no argument that what you eat and drink has significant impacts on vitality, when it comes to cultivating a strong Work Vitality Quotient, activation in the form of physical movement has the most accessible and universal benefits.

Humans are built for motion. Nearly every beneficial mind and body system is optimized through movement. That movement doesn't have to be running a marathon or sweating it out in a HIIT class. It can be anything, such as ping-pong, paddleboarding, or walking. Regardless of how it is produced, activity positively impacts your mental, emotional, and physical energy, whether protecting it, enhancing it, or replenishing it.

While the physical health benefits of exercise are well known, the benefits of exercise on your mental health, overall well-being, and performance have recently become better understood and appreciated. Some of the most relevant implications for accessing activation as a key contribution to a strong Work Vitality Quotient include:

- Decreased screen fatigue

- Reduced anxiety and stress

- Improved attention, learning, and memory

- Better mental flexibility and psychological stamina

- Higher levels of self-confidence, and life and work satisfaction

- A more positive outlook, better emotional regulation, and increased mood stabilization

One of the reasons exercise has such profound effects on our health and well-being is largely due to the fact that it strengthens brain functioning by increasing oxygen levels, blood supply, and important neural growth factor hormones such as BDNF (brain derived neurotrophic factor). BDNF both protects and promotes neural growth—think of it as fertilizer for the brain. One area of the brain that is particularly sensitive to BDNF is in the hippocampus, which you'll recall is critical to emotional regulation, learning, and memory and just so happens to also be highly susceptible to damage by excessive cortisol. While originally thought to only be produced in the brain, new data suggests that contracted skeletal muscles also produce BDNF during exercise. In other words, physical activity directly increases levels of BDNF, which boosts brain function and buffers it from the detrimental wear-and-tear effects of cortisol when stress is high.

With the benefits of exercise so plentiful, and "exercising more" topping the list of activities that would most positively contribute to increasing one's Work Vitality Quotient, why do only a reported quarter of the population meet the guidelines for adequate exercise? The most common objections include simply not liking to exercise or not having enough time, energy, resources, or motivation to do it.

Let's take a moment to unpack these explanations. I have found that most people who say they don't like exercising really mean one or both of the following: they haven't found an exercise they like doing or they don't look forward to exercising. Both of these make sense. For starters, we often associate exercise with going to the gym or sweating it out on the home treadmill. For a bounty of reasons neither of those may be possible or sound enjoyable to you. But exercise also includes recreational sports as well as activities such as swimming, yoga, biking, weight training, hiking, golf, tennis, karate, squash, or dancing in your living room for that matter— whatever movement you enjoy most.

Next, ask anyone who regularly exercises why they do it, and they'll usually focus on its energizing and empowering effect along with its beneficial impact on their effectiveness and health. In other words, they focus on the advantages they experience *as a result* of exercising. Ask those same people if they always *feel* like exercising before starting and you'll get a very different answer.

Activation often requires you to do the opposite of what you feel like doing, especially in the moment. I truly enjoy exercise, and still there are days it's the last thing I feel like doing. As such, when I'm stressed, jet-lagged, tired, truly have too much to do in

For vitality-boosting
practices, focus on how
you want to feel *after*
the experience, not on
what you feel like doing
in the moment.

———————————————

the available hours, or feel that it is coming at the cost of time with my loved ones, it is the first thing I convince myself to skip. The problem is that when it comes to activities and practices that not only refuel us, but help us be the best version of ourselves, we mistakenly start by *focusing on the wrong end of the experience*, or more specifically, we make decisions based on what we feel like doing in the moment. Our comfort-loving, reward-seeking, ease-craving brain will invariably negotiate us out of the actions that are best for us because they usually require an initial investment of effort. As such, the biggest difference between those who exercise regularly and those who don't has less to do with time, energy, motivation, or resources and more to do with where they put their focus. To make the best decisions when it comes to vitality-boosting practices, it helps to focus on what you want to feel *after* the experience. Keep a list of your positive exercise–generated aftereffects and the next time your brain tries to lure you into skipping movement, look at your list for motivation.

While feeling resistant to doing what's hard in the moment is both normal and real, it doesn't mean it's true. As unlikely as it sounds in most situations, *you do have the energy, motivation, and time*—it's just locked up in your muscles. And how do you access these benefits? You guessed it; they are unlocked through movement.

If you've ever said, "I'm going for a walk to clear my head," you intuitively know that movement influences your perceptions and emotions. In addition to the impact of increased oxygen saturation in your blood, blood flow to the brain, and endorphins circulating through the body, something called "endocannabinoids" play an important role in the positive experiences you get from exercise. Endocannabinoids are naturally occurring chemical compounds produced within the body that bind to the same brain receptors as the compounds found in cannabis.

The research is new but preliminary studies suggest that heightened endocannabinoid levels are one key reason why during and after exercising your perspective expands, your outlook brightens, you feel more connected with others, and whatever stresses and struggles you're facing feel more manageable. The connection is that the areas of your brain responsible for these experiences are rich in endocannabinoid receptors. These are feelings and experiences that come *as a result* of movement.

While influenced by a number of factors, exercising for twenty to thirty minutes per day appears to be key in reliably promoting increased BDNF and raising endocannabinoid levels. This means to gain the benefits of exercise, you have to get over the initial challenge of *getting started*, which you probably won't feel like doing. If you push yourself through the first emotionally, mentally, and physically hard part, by staying with it your body rewards you by unlocking the benefits. Simply put, moving your body makes you healthier, stronger, more energized, capable, and resourceful—it makes you feel more alive!

To build more activation into your day, step one is to look for a form of movement you enjoy. Step two is to accept the following: the up-front energy required to start exercise is exponentially returned *after you exercise*. The enhanced motivation comes during exercise, rarely before it, and the time input is repaid in the form of after-exercise efficiencies in performance and health. Add to this, time is one of your most precious assets and prioritizing it for exercise is one of the fastest ways to access your vitality. And step three is actually moving! Have you ever regretted getting up and moving your body for twenty minutes? Ninety-nine percent of the time, you feel substantially better afterward and those around you reap the benefits of this as well. The few times exercise doesn't help you feel better, it still strengthens the trust you have in yourself to follow through on hard things and instills confidence in knowing you did something that will serve you, others, your work, and ultimately your vitality in the future.

Restoration
· · · · · · · · · · · · · ·

Restoration is the next category in the CARE Index. Resting nurtures your mind and body, providing time to think and not. It includes relaxation, sleep, time in nature, and mindful reflection.

While most people say they want more downtime for rest and relaxation, those same people also tend to be quite bad at doing it! It never ceases to amaze me how many people can juggle more things than I could ever keep track of but struggle to slow down when needed. Often it is because we are addicted to doing, producing, and achieving. The reality is that restoration is the opposite of all these things.

Relaxation

Kick back, chill out, decompress, unwind, me-time—people tend to define and desire relaxation differently. While personal, restful relaxation typically involves four elements:

1 Unstructured, accomplishment-free time (also known as to-do list free).

2 Allowing yourself to put your current stressors to the side for the moment.

3 The freedom to choose what you do or don't do in that time.

4 Little active energy going out but lots of nourishing, restorative energy coming in.

Perhaps most importantly, relaxation is a powerful form of recovery when you take the pressure off to relax! The goal isn't to "do" relaxation; the goal is to feel relaxed.

If you only skimmed the paragraph above because you identify as a Type-A person who shudders at the idea of relaxation, then this is especially essential for you. Relaxation allows your brain to find new creative connections that are inaccessible when you are actively engaged in creative brainstorming or problem-solving efforts. Sometimes it's by stopping that you find the best, most innovative way to move forward.

Sleep

If you were to ask my husband about my sleep routine, he'd roll his eyes and claim that I'm an eighty-five-year-old stuck in a middle-aged woman's body. I am not offended by this; I also consider it "eating late" if dinner is after five-thirty, so the description fits. After returning from my trip to Germany, the most significant change I made that still holds true today was regarding sleep. I have specific sleep preparation rituals and rarely shift the hours I go to bed and wake, including getting seven-and-a-half hours of sleep (give or take thirty minutes) a night. Of course, there are exceptions for special events, but sleep is the last thing I willingly sacrifice.

An important disclaimer: I am not at the mercy of a sleep disorder. I do not work shift work hours. I don't have any small children needing my attention in the middle of the night, nor am I in a caretaking role. I also have a safe environment in which to sleep. Even if you can't check off each of these boxes, small adjustments in routines and practices can significantly improve sleep.

For many people, including me, as I learned through my trip to Germany, sleep is an invisible catalyst out of survival mode. When you feel rested, which includes getting enough high-quality hours of sleep, you feel more positive, energized, and resourceful, all the while giving your brain and body the needed time to repair, rewire, and refuel itself for optimal functioning.

While sleep is linked to improved cognitive function, including focus, learning, creativity, and strategic thought, I suspect few would disagree: When you are sleep deprived, everything feels harder and takes longer. The influence of fear, obligation, and guilt are more potently felt. You think less efficiently, make decisions less strategically, communicate less empathetically, all while your attention fragments and your patience frays. If you've ever just accepted a meeting or commitment because you were too tired to effectively say no or negotiate in the moment, you know the influence fatigue can have.

Much of this can be chalked up to the fact that when sleep deprived, the amygdala becomes less discerning and more sensitive to negative stimuli, heightening the risk of being swept away by your emotions. Research by Matthew Walker and others out of the University of California, Berkeley, found that sleep helps soften the edges of sharp emotions, while helping expand both your perspective and the ability to see the upside of challenges. This is why we say, "Sleep on it; things will look different in the morning"— because it is true. Sleep can make something that seems impossible today seem a little more possible tomorrow.

Time in Nature

"Go outside; it's good for you." No, this isn't just something parents say to kids to get them out of their hair. The science backs it up: nature has powerful restorative effects. Being in nature can help you simultaneously feel both relaxed and energized. Focused and creative. Alive and calm. A series of six studies looking at the impact of nature on vitality published in the *Journal of Environmental Psychology* found that it took a mere twenty minutes a day outdoors to significantly boost vitality levels. Other studies have found that our blood pressure and resting heart rate can be lower in as little as five minutes in nature. Even patients having a window that looks out at a natural environment tend to show better rates of recovery.

Next time you head out to hike a nature trail or go for a walk in the park, leave the earphones at home. Focus on slowing down your breath and pay attention to take in your surroundings with as many of your senses as possible. Without the buzzes, bright screens, and constant stimulation, activity in the prefrontal cortex decreases and stabilizes, allowing you to fully take in the restorative benefits. There is a good reason why it is said that nature is fuel for the soul.

Mindful Reflection

For years I've taught courses in leadership both directly to organizations and as part of executive education programs. Daily, the leaders in these courses faced an unprecedented volume of incoming information, demands on their time, and decisions needing to be made. One of the first questions I'd ask at the start was, "What is one thing that would help you be a better leader?" The answer wasn't surprising: time. In particular, time to *think more*—reflect, plan, and strategize.

Shortly after, these same leaders would receive a 360-degree leadership feedback assessment with dedicated, undisturbed time to read it, reflect, and debrief with a coach. Yet, without fail, the leaders would quickly scan through the feedback and immediately pick up their phones and begin scrolling.

Why? You might think it's because of a need to be on 24/7. But the truth is that, as much as people say they want more time to think, and as unenjoyable as most people say it is to spend the day putting out fires, it is often more comfortable to be reactive than to be reflective. Being annoyed with an email is easier then contemplating hard feedback.

These leaders had the information; they just needed to slow down long enough to consider how to best use it. Most of us in our daily lives repeat the same pattern. We face challenging, frustrating, and often exhausting days, and instead of stepping back to reflect and learn from them, we just head into the next day, hoping things will be different.

Through my research, one of the most striking differences between those who feel perpetually locked in survival mode and those who work more consistently in their stand-out zone is having a regular mindfulness or self-reflection practice. That could be meditation, prayer, daily journaling, reflecting on joy and gratitude, or undisturbed time to plan for the future or learn from the past. Not only does it help you learn and grow, but neuroscientists find that mindfulness influences brain areas related to perception, body awareness, emotional regulation, introspection, and complex thought.

Laughing, learning,
having fun, and
engaging in hobbies
do not divert you from
success; they are
a road to it.

Being mindful with your attention, energy, and behaviors is both the simplest and greatest gift you can give to others and to yourself.

Exploration

The final category of the CARE Index is exploration. When was the last time you purposefully did something new? What was the last thing you learned? How long has it been since you last laughed at yourself—not in judgment, but in joyful appreciation for your willingness to suck at something and keep trying it anyway?

Exploration is about tapping into your brain's natural inclination to explore, seek out new experiences, learn and master interests, engage in hobbies, and infuse a sense of fun and play into your life. It engages your brain's "seeking system," which as you know, motivates you to approach the world with a vitality-rich sense of wonder. It pushes you to pursue a hobby like salsa dancing just because you enjoy it even if you're terrible at it or attend Toastmasters to overcome your fear of public speaking.

Learning

Learning is perhaps the most innate human behavior and an invigorating one at that. Learning and working are not the same. And yet, if you've ever had a stressed-out colleague who's begrudgingly been "sent" to a professional development course, only to return refreshed and excited to talk about and try out the new ideas they learned, then you've witnessed how connected they can be.

Not only does learning expand your knowledge, but it strengthens your brain. Recent research has shown that in addition to having positive relationships, engaging in regular exercise, and getting enough sleep, lifelong learning is also a powerful line of defense protecting your brain from cognitive decline and associated impairments. So take a course online, learn to home brew craft beer, watch a documentary, read about history, practice identifying the birds in your backyard, or exercise your brain with the latest Wordle—just never stop learning.

Hobbies

One *big* assumption about burnout is that it comes from working too much. Although too much work without adequate rest and recovery most certainly will have an impact, burnout is often rooted in feeling powerless, which is why workplace culture dynamics play such a significant role. And while we can't necessarily change the culture of our workplace, studies show that hobbies can provide us with a sense of control, serve as a positive and effective distraction, and provide an outlet to authentically express ourselves.

Hobbies are simply activities—separate from your work—that you willingly choose and enjoy doing. While some hobbies involve learning, competition, and personal betterment, you don't have to be good at them, nor do they need to serve any bigger purpose, any person, or have any real value for that matter.

They also serve another important function—they are diversifiers. For example, hobbies diversify your identity. If you love your work, feel fulfilled by it, and truly don't feel like you need to "recover" from your day, then outside interests and hobbies might be even more important. As you've learned, what you do for work can morph into representing who you are. Hobbies can expand your self-image if you do things different from your work. You can be an entrepreneur and a pickleball player. A sales manager and a drummer.

Hobbies are diversifiers of energy and purpose. Some days will inevitably be hard, setbacks will occur, and confidence will be diminished. When all your focus is on your work, these experiences can temporarily leave you feeling worthless and lost. Without a buffer of other interests, these feelings can be mistaken for facts. When you have hobbies to invest your time and attention into, they can give you a supplemented sense of purpose, as well as exposure to alternative perspectives. They also provide you with a healthy achievement outlet. Not to mention that when you have limited time outside of work, investing in hobbies has been shown to help people feel more restored, feel more creative and capable, and get into a relaxed state more quickly.

Finally, hobbies diversify your social circles as they often connect people around a shared interest. A sense of community is a powerful thing, and as you've learned, doing things collectively with others can amplify joy. If you love the work you do and feel fulfilled by doing it, the best way to protect that commitment and passion is to ensure that work is not the only thing that makes you happy—think of hobbies as happiness diversifiers.

Play and Fun

I have long believed that when we laugh, we let love in. Laughter makes us feel alive. And yet, according to the Association for Applied and Therapeutic Humor, children laugh around 300 times a day, whereas adults laugh between 3 and 20 times a day. A significant contributor to this drastic difference is that kids just play more and thus have more laughter-provoking fun. Earlier, we talked about "funtegration"—when you integrate something fun to something you find stressful or undesirable. And while striving for 300 moments of laughter a day may not be a realistic goal, incorporating more experiences that provoke it is possible.

Think of playful fun as doing something for recreational enjoyment that you don't need to be good at and that allows you to let your guard down—and it's even better if it makes you laugh. When you allow your creativity and imagination to open up, you'll find that fun and play are the quickest routes to feeling a sense of freedom from the demands of the world.

I wrote this chapter on a Sunday afternoon in winter. The bay behind my house was frozen over and the ice was in great shape for skating. My husband was out playing pick-up hockey with people from the neighborhood. I could hear them laughing from my office, and I couldn't help but smile. I could also predict the first thing he would say when he walked in the door: "That was fun." As a result, he'd head into work Monday morning feeling more restored.

Laughing, having fun, learning about the world, and engaging in hobbies do not divert you from success; they are a road to it.

15

CARE at Work

IT'S EIGHT-THIRTY in the morning and you have a jammed schedule ahead of you. Which approach do you choose? Do you take small, dedicated breaks throughout the workday, leaving you with energy at the end to re-engage with the important people and interests in your life?

BUT not get everything done that you feel you should.

Or do you push hard straight through the day, using any opportunity for a break to get more done, leaving you drained by the end with little energy to re-engage with the important people and interests in your life?

BUT not get everything done that you feel you should.

You did not read that wrong. Either way, you won't get everything done that you feel you should. That is the reality of the world of work today. And still, that's the benchmark most of us measure ourselves against. In response, we push through the day, overriding breaks and burning through our energy reserves.

There is plenty of inarguable evidence that confirms that taking breaks for CARE throughout your workday directly influences your experiences and performance at work. The benefits range from better productivity output due to improved attention, creativity, and thinking, to providing renewed motivation and making your work more enjoyable. Breaks also reduce decision fatigue, stress, and end-of-day exhaustion.

And still, a survey by the online scheduling platform company Doodle found that despite 72 percent of workers reporting that proactively blocking out times for breaks in their calendar makes them feel less burned out, only 14 percent say they actually do it.

Unfortunately, the repercussions of break-free days also spill into life outside of work. In a 360-degree leadership survey I conducted with a senior team of a professional service firm, those who self-assessed as being least likely to designate time for breaks in the day were also assessed by their friends and family as being less mentally or emotionally present outside of work.

While constant meetings, heavy workloads, and general workplace cultural norms are significant contributors to the lack of workday breaks, how can we start to turn the tables on this trend?

When it comes to Work Vitality Quotient–boosting breaks there are two things to consider to effectively get us started: the quantity of time taken for a break, and the quality of actions taken during the break. Never underestimate the value and impact of short, high-quality breaks taken consistently over time.

Quantity of Time for Breaks

Have you ever been forced to take a cold shower? If the answer is yes, even if it only took two minutes to slather on soap and shampoo your hair, it probably still felt like an eternity. And yet taking a break that would have replenishing effects in under two minutes sounds impossible (even though that cold shower would certainly liven you up!). Given the busyness of our days, many of us feel like we don't have enough time to take a break that would actually make a difference.

I'm sure few would disagree that if you are about to go under the knife for a surgical procedure, you want the best surgeon. It turns out that being the best isn't just about skills. In a small study, researchers from the University of Sherbrooke wanted to see if short, real-time breaks taken during surgery would benefit the performance and energy of surgeons. The experiment tested the impact of twenty-second breaks taken every twenty minutes throughout a two-hour operation compared to surgeons who worked straight through the procedure. The short break consisted of mentally and physically disengaging from work by stepping back from the operating table, followed by a simple set of stretches for twenty seconds. To assess the impact of the breaks, levels of physical strength and accuracy were assessed before and after the surgery. In addition, surgeons' self-reported levels of physical discomfort were assessed.

While a twenty-second break seems negligible, surgeons who took them were seven times more accurate in the assessment after the surgery than those who didn't. Just to be clear, accuracy levels were incredibly high in both scenarios; however, any improvements only lower the chance of complications.

Perhaps most notably, those who took breaks reported less pain in their back, neck, shoulders, and wrists. In the physical strength assessments, they demonstrated half the level of fatigue by the end of the surgery. The benefits of increased stamina and physical comfort compounded over a shift can be the difference between these surgeons ending the day with energy for their families and interests or not.

The Microboosters

Our brains and bodies are optimized to work in higher-impact surges, broken up by short breaks. You can do this by implementing what I call "microboosters." Microboosters are short twenty-second to ten-minute breaks taken consistently throughout the day that provide boosts of energy.

Examples can include something as simple as taking two minutes to close your eyes, relax your muscles, and breathe. Send a message or call someone you love. Listen to a favorite song. Chat with a coworker. Make a cup of herbal tea. Do one minute of jumping jacks or simply stand up at your desk and stretch for twenty seconds. On days when it feels like there is no time for anything, my go-to microbooster is to drink more water to help me feel more energized, think more clearly, and focus more effectively.

Remember, your brain tends to believe that how you feel in the moment is how you'll feel in the future. As such, you are biased to rationalize that small actions won't make a big enough difference, which to be clear, is untrue. Add in the tendency to think in all-or-nothing terms when feeling overwhelmed and suddenly you're discounting taking any break at all. For example, if you don't have the luxury of a full hour to get out of the office for lunch, your brain will try to negotiate you into working through the time available while eating at your desk. Remember that *everything counts*. As my trainer once told me, "The ten-minute walk you did do is always better than the intended forty-five-minute exercise class you didn't do."

Take a moment and review the CARE Index you captured and the list of activities you've brainstormed for each category—connection, activation, restoration, and exploration. Now break down each category further by first listing as many microbooster practices (the smallest version of a practice) you can think of—nothing is too small. Second, reflect on the factors that make for a wildly busy day and brainstorm ways to make your microboosters as accessible as possible.

Perhaps this goes without saying, but the easiest first step is proactively blocking time for breaks in your schedule. For my fellow hangry people (those who get a little gnarly with others when hungry), this might be as significant as doing some meal prep. That way if you only have five minutes to grab some lunch, something healthy is at your fingertips. It might be pre-planning the online workout

Microboosters
are short breaks
taken consistently
throughout the day
that boost energy.

———————————

you will do so you don't waste time trying to figure it out in the moment. If you work in a meeting-heavy environment, schedule meetings for fifty minutes to have a ten-minute buffer. One of the most powerful practices to increase the likelihood of taking breaks is having an accountability partner at work. You can support one another with a positive reminder nudge to take a break.

There is one caveat to microboosters that is important to consider. While taking a few microbooster breaks throughout the day is better than none when things are chaotic, depending on how taxing your work is—mentally, emotionally, or physically—they may not be enough to keep you in the stand-out zone over the long run.

Quality of Breaks Taken

Not all activities have the same vitality-boosting effect. When breaks are only in reaction to feeling frustrated, tired, or in an attempt to distract ourselves, we often end up engaging in activities that add to those negative experiences rather than CARE-focused practices that relieve us or replenish our energy.

Consider the differences: You connect with a colleague to catch up or brainstorm ideas for an upcoming project—that can boost energy. Simply venting about how much everything and everyone sucks does not. Finishing off your third bottle of water is hydrating and energizing; gulping down your eighth cup of coffee for the day is not. Taking a short break to watch a funny video can fill your brain and body with lasting feel-good chemicals; mindlessly scrolling news feeds that worry and anger you does not.

The POWER Boosters

With time being a precious commodity, tapping into a simple set of high-quality practices that you can draw on quickly and flexibly throughout your day is critical. Five practices, in particular, amplify your Work Vitality Quotient to help you contribute to your highest-value work. I call these "POWER boosters":

- Permission granting to pause
- Oxygenating
- Walking
- Energy KVI check-in
- Resetting

While each separately can be a microbooster, putting these POWER boosters into a single break can increase the cumulative effect by helping you better assess if the way you are working is working.

Permission Granting to Pause

There will always be something that requires your attention. As much as you believe that time and circumstances are the biggest obstacles in taking breaks, often the most significant hindrance is *you*. You need to give yourself the permission to actually stop and mentally, emotionally, and physically disengage from your work. Permission requires overcoming the initial resistance to breaks created by your brain. Your relationship to work and the beliefs you hold about what drives success can muddy the water. Permit yourself to feel whatever emotions come up when you think of taking a break (including fear, obligation, guilt). Thank them for trying to keep you safe and comfortable, and then let them know you choose to challenge yourself to do what is most needed to bring your best—and that requires a break.

Oxygenating

While it's highly unlikely anyone has ever said, "Give me a moment, I need to oxygenate," that's perhaps the most accurate description

Creating space to
reset your perspective
is at the heart of
cultivating a strong
Work Vitality Quotient.

of this POWER booster. When I say "oxygenate," I mean literally take a moment to fill your body with more oxygen.

Allow me to get a little nerdy for a moment; not all breathing has the same effect. You can be intentional and use your breath to create specific effects, known as breath work. For starters, you can use your breath to increase your energy by simply breathing in slowly through your nose. Your sinuses produce a molecule called nitric oxide. When you breathe in through your nose, the nitric oxide helps to open up blood vessels, increasing circulating oxygen levels in your blood. The higher the oxygen saturation of your blood, the more refreshed and energized you feel. You breathe to stay alive but *you oxygenate to feel alive.*

Intentionally slowing down and deepening your breath has other benefits as well. For example, lengthening and deepening your breath rate can influence your stress response and create a calming effect. To initiate this response, it is generally agreed that slowing your breath rate to six breaths a minute (five-second inhales followed by a five-second exhale) for a few consecutive minutes is a good benchmark. In as little as two minutes, you can physiologically start applying the brake on your stress response, creating the environment for your cortisol levels to begin dropping back to their healthy baseline. Remember, cortisol is healthy in short bursts. It's when levels stay high that the deleterious wear-and-tear effects take hold. If you are feeling anxious, nervous, or emotionally triggered by something like a negative customer review on your company's website, a slightly longer exhale helps slow your heart rate. By proactively choosing to oxygenate throughout the day, you regain a sense of control and lessen the compounding effect cortisol has on your system.

While slowing down and deepening your breath helps to regulate your stress response, a lack of oxygen or shallow breathing has the opposite effect. For many, a significant amount of time is spent sitting in front of screens. If this is you, then the chances are high that you are a part of the estimated 80 percent of the population that unconsciously holds their breath or falls into shallow breathing when engaged in email. This phenomenon is so prevalent that it even has its own name, "email apnea," first coined by Linda Stone in a 2008 *Huffington Post* article. The challenge is that when you hold your breath or breathe in a shallow or quick sequence, you inadvertently activate your stress response—even in the absence of actual stress! More recently, research has found that we tend to do this whenever we are in front of screens in general, including during videoconference calls.

As a vitality-boosting practice all on its own, intentional breath work is the most accessible strategy you have at your disposal and yet is also the most underutilized. The reality is that you have to breathe anyway! You might as well breathe in a way that helps you.

Walking

Walking requires no preparation, no equipment, and can be expanded or contracted to any available time frame. It is perhaps the most versatile POWER booster, especially considering on average, office-based workers are reported to spend 75 percent of their workday sitting, with much of that time spent in prolonged, unbroken bouts. The percentage is likely higher if you work from a home office.

Studies have shown you can prolong concentration, creativity, memory, and focus just by walking more throughout the day. If you have the time, head outside and see if you can find a nice tree-lined street. Remember, nature provides your hardworking, mentally fatigued prefrontal cortex some offline rest. Even better, ask a friend to join and focus on topics of conversation that invoke joy and connection. Add a bit of exploration and head down a safe street or path you've never been down, and now you've incorporated each element of CARE for maximal benefits.

Energy KVI Check-In

An energy check-in means taking a moment to assess your energy levels—mentally, emotionally, and physically—against your Key

Vitality Indicators (KVIs). Remember, the goal of monitoring your KVIs is to learn to decode what your mind and body are communicating to you about your energy. Perhaps one of the most understated opportunities of an energy check-in is that it allows you to extend your stamina by noticing when you are using more energy than is required. We tend to hold emotions in our bodies; that shows up as muscle tension, which is tremendously energy expensive. Use your physical energy check-in as a reminder to scan your body for tension and relax your muscles.

Depending on stress levels and energy reserves, energy check-ins are also an opportunity to watch out for any KVI red flags and adjust. The busier you are, the less likely you will notice changes in your energy and behavior without intentional monitoring. Otherwise, you only notice when you end up with a blazing headache, overreact to something negligible, mindlessly forget an important appointment, or lose your phone. The skill is catching yourself *before* you experience these repercussions, and the way to do this is with regular energy KVI check-ins.

Resetting

In an article for *Harvard Business Review*, Brigid Schulte explains that when we're busy and feeling tight on time, "our attention and ability to focus narrows. Behavioral researchers call this phenomenon 'tunneling.' And, like being in a tunnel, we can only concentrate on the most immediate, and often low value tasks right in front of us, with some research suggesting we actually lose about 13 IQ points in this state." The final POWER booster aims to snap us out of this tunnel view by resetting our perspective to help us take on a more expanded, stand-out zone view.

Whereas reflection is the action of looking back on a situation to better understand what happened after the fact, resetting occurs in the moment. It is the process of compassionately challenging your current outlook with agency-creating questions. It involves getting curious about your feelings, motives, interpretations, and circumstances and examining how they influence your perspectives and reactions. The goal of resetting is to look for alternative possibilities that help get you back into or keep you in the stand-out zone.

In 2020, a group of researchers was interested in understanding why some people working at a law firm could achieve a satisfying work-life balance even though their colleagues found it difficult. To carry out the study, researchers included an even gender split among respondents. All were between the ages of thirty and fifty, had a least one dependent child, were in a management role, and were meeting performance expectations. Half of the study sample were employees who reported a perceived pressure to work long hours as the biggest contributor to their lack of work-life balance. The other half felt the same pressure but resisted working long hours and, as expected, reported higher satisfaction with their work-life balance.

It turns out that the biggest difference with the group that experienced better work-life balance was their commitment to continually reset their thinking. This meant examining their experience of feeling pressured to work long hours and challenging their assumptions about what was actually required to meet the demands. For example, instead of automatically working later when an end-of-the-day request landed on their desk they would stop and ask themselves, "How else could I address this request that doesn't require sacrificing my time with loved ones and personal priorities?" The by-product of thinking in assumption-challenging, possibility-generating ways was more creative problem-solving. What distinguished these employees was they accepted that each day required resets to make adjustments and experiment with potentially different strategies to sustain their work-life satisfaction.

The good news is that you've been building the skill of resetting throughout this book. Each time you've tapped into your wonder circuitry and asked yourself agency-creating questions to rethink your beliefs about success, stress, and rest, you've practiced resetting. Other examples of stand-out zone resets include asking yourself the following:

- What is my role or contribution to what is happening right now?

- Is this a comfort-driven choice or challenge-embracing choice?

- How might the emotions of fear, obligation, or guilt be influencing my decisions?

- Is this me getting ensnared in a success trap that I know doesn't serve me?

- What resources can I draw on to best address the stress in this moment?

- What would best serve my ability to sustainably work from my stand-out zone?

It likely won't surprise you that one of my most-used resetting questions is, "What actions can I take right now that will help ensure those who deserve the best of me get it?" Creating space to reset your perspective is at the heart of cultivating a strong Work Vitality Quotient.

What we do during the day will most certainly influence how energized we feel at the end of the day. Add to this that from a brain-design perspective, what your brain does consistently is what your brain does efficiently. If you train yourself, and therefore your brain, to efficiently disconnect from work stressors with CARE breaks during the day, it will also be easier to do outside of work.

16

CARE Away from Work

"WHAT do you do in your free time?" That is the question that resulted in a total brain freeze for Halim. Not the kind you get from drinking a slushie. The kind you get when you can't think of anything meaningful to say. At a loss for a good answer, he jokingly responded, "I'd need to *have* free time to do something with it!"

Driving home from work later that day, Halim found himself unable to stop thinking about the question. If his colleague had asked, "What do you do outside of work?" he would have been able to rhyme off a list of things. He runs errands, does household chores, chauffeurs kids to various activities, and takes his aging parents to appointments. He tries to squeeze in time to play squash, and he gets away for a fishing trip once a year. But the idea of *free time* felt so foreign that Halim simply blanked. Chances are, you probably see some of yourself in Halim's story.

In general, and especially when we feel stressed and tired, we aren't all that strategic, creative, or discerning about how we use our free time. Following the same reasoning of why we don't take more breaks during the workday, most of us don't feel like we have enough free time outside of work and believe that whatever time we do have should be used productively. Not surprisingly, doing things we enjoy tends to be the first things to fall off our list.

The Belief of Not Having Enough Free Time

In his 2017 TED talk, Adam Alter, a professor of marketing at New York University's Stern School of Business, shared his research on the effect of digital devices on our health, happiness, and use of time. Taking Alter's data into account and corroborating it with others' work on how our time is dispersed over an average day, we find that:

- Sleep accounts for approximately seven-and-a-half hours.

- Work plus commuting accounts for approximately nine hours.

- Life-essential activities such as preparing meals, eating, bathing, taking care of kids, and household chores account for three to four hours.

This breakdown of time leaves somewhere between three to four hours of free personal time a day. Some days, time is scarce. Some seasons of our lives are busier than others. Access to resources, predictability in work schedules, financial stability, and caretaking responsibilities can significantly impact how much free time someone has. Taking all that into account, we generally still have more space in our day for nourishing, restoring, and reinvigorating CARE practices than we believe. The bigger questions are, how can we best use our free time and where are we losing opportunities for it?

It turns out that the amount of free time we have has remained relatively stable over the last decade and a half. What has changed is how we use that time—and I suspect what is contributing to that change won't surprise anyone. Screen time has steadily and dramatically been gobbling up our free time. Who hasn't gone on their phone to look something up only to get pulled into a scroll-hole? You know this has happened if you look up from your phone only to notice that twenty minutes has unknowingly passed and you still haven't actually looked up the information you wanted when you picked up your phone in the first place.

Of course, some of our device use is essential, enriching, and enjoyable. Still, Alter's data suggests that we spend three times longer mindlessly engaging with things that drain our energy and cause us to lose track of time. This includes watching things that anger, sadden, or demotivate us. But it's not just our digital devices getting in the way of making the most of our free time; other culprits are also at play.

The Belief That Free Time Should Be Productive Time

Have you ever found yourself nearing the end of a hectic week, counting down the hours until you can just relax? Then the weekend arrives, and soon the goal of relaxing is replaced with a feeling of restlessness and guilt. Next thing you know, you find yourself thinking, "Well, if I'm not doing anything important, I might as well get some work done." I call this phenomenon the "might-as-well mentality," and it kicks in the moment you stop feeling busy and start feeling uncomfortable. Even though you need (and want) a break, once available, your brain attempts to lure you back into the comfort zone of what feels normal and easy. As counterintuitive as it sounds, for many, it is more comfortable to feel stressed, be reactive, and tend to the needs of others than it is to feel at peace, be proactive, and focus on activities to recharge your batteries and refuel your spirit.

Other times, it may not be the pull of work at all. Perhaps it's what happens in those instances when life invites you to just be, such as spending the afternoon playing at the park with your kids. Even while recognizing these are special moments and the kids are growing up fast, once there, you can't shake the conflicted feeling that you're losing valuable time by just playing when the bathroom grout needs scrubbing, and the lawn needs mowing. The incessant and internally driven pressure to prioritize productivity makes it feel impossible to be present and enjoy the moments of simply living.

As you've discovered over the course of this book, our beliefs and mindsets have a crucial role in how we perceive and experience the world—and our free time outside of work is no exception. A 2021 study led by Gabriela Tonietto of Rutgers Business School had participants fill out a series of questionnaires to assess their percep- tions of free time, which in the study was labeled leisure time. She included questions such as, "How much do you agree that time spent on leisure activities is often wasted time?" Between ques- tionnaires, participants were given downtime where they watched four different popular YouTube videos rated as entertaining or funny by a separate group of people. Those who had assessed leisure as a waste of time on the questionnaire also rated the videos as less entertaining than those who believed leisure was important.

Even though this is a very simple study, the implications are broad and deserve consideration. If you believe leisure is a waste of time, it likely will be. Not because it isn't helpful or needed, but because your mindset toward leisure undermines its mental, emotional, and physical health benefits. Add to this, those who associated leisure with laziness and believed all time should be used productively also self-reported higher levels of stress, anxiety, and burnout and lower levels of fun, fulfillment, and happiness.

And yet, even if you wholeheartedly believe that focusing exclusively on work is a fast track to burnout and that our cultural obsession with productivity is toxic, many of us still struggle to tip the overworking, under-living balance.

Author and philosopher Frédéric Lenoir said, "Existence is a fact, but living is an art." Art doesn't just happen, it takes effort, skill, and intention.

The incessant
pressure to prioritize
productivity makes
it feel impossible
to be present and enjoy
the moments
of simply living.

To boost your Work Vitality Quotient and feel more alive in all areas of your life, I have pulled five of the most consistent findings from my research to help you carve out revitalizing free time. In short, it helps to:

1   Reframe free time into meaningful time.

2   Free up time with rituals and boundaries.

3   Balance your to-do list with a to-live list.

4   Diversify your free-time activities.

5   Take the pressure off your time off.

Reframe Free Time into Meaningful Time

Yes, it feels like you have less time, more demands, and often impossible expectations to meet, which makes the idea of focusing on CARE in your limited free time feel less accessible. You also know that the brain is motivated by meaning. By tethering the need for free time to something meaningful, you are less likely to be pulled off course by outdated success beliefs or the coercive influence of fear, obligation, and guilt. To do this, simply take your brain's free-time objections and reframe them positively and purposefully. Some examples include:

• Instead of seeing free time as a wasted opportunity for productivity, reframe it as an investment in future you, your relationships, joy, and success.

• Instead of singularly focusing on your work ethic, partner it with a rest ethic to ensure you can make your highest contribution, stay aligned with your values, prioritize your health and well-being, and ultimately tip the balance of overworking and under-living.

- Instead of seeing free time as optional, reframe it as a non-negotiable way to ensure the people who deserve the best of you, including yourself, actually get it.

These are not trade-offs to great work; they are drivers of it.

Free Up Free Time with Rituals and Boundaries

Sabine Sonnentag, professor of psychology at the University of Mannheim, has studied workplace wellness and suggests four key elements that most significantly contribute to a good, restorative break or vacation.

- We need some time for rest and relaxation.

- We need to do something that provides a sense of mastery, learning, or accomplishment.

- We need to have control or a sense of freedom in how we use some of our break time.

- We need the ability to disengage both physically and psychologically from work or current stressors—or simply put, to be able to switch off from work.

While most of us appreciate the need to disconnect physically from work, mentally and emotionally disconnecting is another story. Doing so requires recognizing an important distinction—not actively working is not the same as resting. If you've ever been called out for checking your work phone while out with others, and your reply has been, "I'm not working, I'm just checking!" Ahem, this still counts as working.

Whether keeping an eye on email or ruminating about work, you miss many of the benefits of free time when you need them

To shift out of
overworking and
under-living, balance
your to-do list with
a to-live list.

———————

the most. As Anne Lamott said, "Almost everything will work again if you unplug it for a few minutes, including you."

To make detaching from work more accessible, it helps to work with the brain's natural design. Your brain wants to conserve energy, so it defaults to habits and is motivated by consistency. You can provide each by implementing rituals and boundaries.

Rituals to cue your brain that it's time to disengage from work and re-engage in a different area of life could include:

- Changing out of work clothes.

- Shutting down the computer, turning off lights, closing the office door.

- If working from a shared space at home, closing the laptop's lid and moving it out of sight. For example, putting it in a drawer, in a different room, or covering it with a blanket.

- Establishing "no work" zones in the house, such as the bedroom or while sitting on your favorite comfy chair.

- If commuting, using that time to purposely decompress, read, or listen to something enjoyable.

One of my favorite examples is from a woman whose fabric store was closed during the 2020 pandemic. She set up a digital store from her home but realized she missed the act of opening and closing the store. She bought an open/closed sign and hung it on the home office door, flipping it to open at the start of the day and flipping it to closed to transition into the evening.

Establishing boundaries for your digital devices is essential to get the most out of your free time and keep mindless phone scrolling at bay. It can be as simple as establishing no-phone zones such as at dinner table or during movie night, or putting your phone on airplane mode or turning notifications off when you want to be present. Physically, keep it out of sight when you don't actively need it during the workday. Something as simple as putting it behind you and out of reach can intercept the habit of constantly picking up your phone and mindlessly scrolling—especially when you have something or someone in front of you who deserves your undivided attention.

Set time limits and monitor your usage. Establish specific times when you will go online to check things such as email, and as importantly, when you won't. This will help create longer periods of free time to invest in CARE practices. Not only this, it turns out you feel you have more free time when you have longer uninterrupted periods of time. Two periods with the most potent vitality-boosting potential are limiting time on your phone in the first hour after waking and the final hour before bed. Bringing awareness to how you spend your time is the best way to reclaim it.

Balance Your To-Do List with a To-Live List
. . . .

Although perhaps paradoxical, to make the most of your free time, you need to schedule it in and plan how best to use that time. The mistake many of us make is that we are reactive. We assume a pocket of time will open, and when it does, we assume we'll know how to best use it. Neither happen without intentionality. While your first instinct may be to start making a to-do list, remember that accomplishing tasks is not the same as living a full life. To better tip the balance from overworking and under-living, be as strategic with your energy and experiences as you are with your goals and tasks. Swap out your to-do list and instead make a *to-live list*.

A to-live list is simply a list of special CARE activities or adventures that make you feel alive. Some may be simple, free, and require little pre-planning but are potent aliveness ignitors such as watching the sunset from your favorite park or mountain biking with your family. Others may need more planning and time. These may include aspirational experiences, such as things you've always wanted to try (e.g., take a dance lesson, go zip-lining, or attend a silent meditation retreat); unconventional or special, memorable experiences (e.g., join a Habitat for Humanity build, rent a convert-ible car for a road trip, go whale watching, or take your grandparents to a musical); or once-in-a-lifetime bucket-list experiences (e.g., explore the glaciers of Alaska or ride the tallest roller coaster).

There are no wrong answers here. The goal is to have a list of milestones that will enrich your life, that you can look forward to doing, intentionally plan for, and then actively schedule in. Aim to create space for one adventure a month. Some may be bigger than others but by the end of the year, you will have done twelve memorable things to shift from under-living to fully living. The only risk to this list is if you start treating it like a to-do list. This is not a one-and-done list. There is no pass or fail, good or bad, race or competition to cross things off. The goal isn't to be too structured and goal-oriented with your free time, but to help you make space for it and use it to its fullest potential.

Diversify Your Free-Time Activities

In one interview for this book, I spoke with a gentleman named Greg. He was happy with work and had a nicely balanced CARE Index. He had strong relationships. He was training for a couple of marathons he'd run four years in a row and had a solid sleep and daily prayer routine. Greg always wanted to play the guitar growing up, so he took lessons on Tuesday and Thursday evenings after work.

On paper, he was doing it all right. I was just about to congrat-ulate him when he shared the next part of his story. In a sad twist, a person from his neighborhood went missing, and the police sus-pected it involved foul play. Although Greg was never considered a suspect, investigators talked to each of the residents in the follow-ing months, asking if they'd noticed anything strange and where they were at the time of the suspected crime.

As Greg recounted the story, he shared, "I could tell the police where I would have been because my weeks virtually looked identi-cal, so I knew I was at guitar lessons. I should have felt relieved, but

I kept trying to think about something that specifically stood out on that date, but each week just melded into one. I'm not complaining; I am very grateful because I know I have a wonderful life, but I'm not sure it's a memorable one."

Greg was routined and disciplined and loved to challenge himself. This structure helped him to do and accomplish a lot of different things. Most of us aim for this! And yet, at one point or another, we've all become disillusioned, bored, or creatively drained with work and life. Even when you love what you do and have the economic means to support your passions, as you've learned, sustaining a feeling of aliveness requires a diversity of experiences, but more specifically—elements of spontaneity and novelty. These elements were what was missing for Greg; although he covered activities from each CARE category, they were the same things, done within a goal-focused, ritualized structure week after week.

When every day feels the same, it's hard for any particular day to stand out. It's the novelty of different or unexpected experiences that helps to create memories. Memories then expand our perception of time and differentiate one day from another. A 2016 *Scientific American* article explains it beautifully: "Our retrospective judgment of time is based on how many new memories we create over a certain period. In other words, the more novel memories we build on a weekend getaway, the longer that trip will seem in hindsight."

A healthy brain flourishes on challenge and needs change, even uninvited or unplanned change. It is in the willingness to experiment with new things, especially things that you aren't naturally skilled at, that you often uncover passions and interests that you didn't even know you had. Add to this, novelty and spontaneity are not only memory-builders but potent aliveness activators as well.

Take the Pressure Off Your Time Off

The data is clear: without sufficient recovery periods, it becomes incredibly challenging to maintain performance and enthusiasm for

If you consider
skipping vacation,
ask yourself:
a year from now,
what will I remember
best, the meetings
I attended or
the vacation I took?

---

your work. With stress and burnout levels so high, why do so many people leave unused vacation days each year—even when they get paid time off?

A 2018 annual report released by the US Travel Association on the state of American vacations revealed that workloads were one of the most significant deterrents to people using all of their allotted vacation days. Whether that means not feeling supported to take a break, having too much work to come back to, having no one to cover their work while away, or simply feeling unable to perform their job if they take time off work.

While these concerns are all valid, the same reasons we feel we can't take vacations are what makes taking them so important. Unsurprisingly, I find that those most entrenched in the survival zone are the same people who negate taking holidays. Skipping vacation when you most need it is like feeling barely able to keep your head above water, being thrown a life preserver, and instead of grabbing on to catch your breath and rest your body, you just throw it back, all the while fighting to stay afloat as the waves around you get bigger and bigger. Most troubling is that those who leave vacation unused typically understand the consequences, but the rationalization of the might-as-well mentality, "What's the point? It won't make a difference; I might as well just work" wins out. I understand the sentiment, and it is important to recognize that taking a vacation won't fix work, but it was never meant to.

The Cure-All Pressure

We've put too much pressure on vacations. What we do outside work won't necessarily fix what's happening inside it. No matter how long and restorative your vacation is, it will not change your work culture. Bad boss? Sorry, your vacation doesn't make them more supportive. Conflicting priorities? Yup, they will still be conflicting when you return. When you tie your reasons for taking a vacation to making work better, you set yourself up for disappointment. Instead, recognize that yes, work will still be the same when you return from vacation—but *you* won't be. You will be better able to put things into perspective and to resiliently take on the inevitable challenges with your best, most rested foot forward.

The Timing Pressure

We put pressure on vacations in other ways as well. They become the thing that we put off until the timing is right. When you're not so busy, when the kids are older, when you get the promotion, when you retire—then you'll go on your dream vacation. If you are lucky, you get to do everything you planned. But as we all know, the future is never guaranteed.

I have fallen into the trap of overwork on too many occasions to count. My father has always reminded me of the value of experiences, the longevity of memories, and the importance of taking a vacation now instead of putting it off for the future.

I am grateful he was one to take his own advice. My parents had a lot of plans for how they would grow old together. Unfortunately, they didn't get to see them through because of my mother's passing. As heartbreaking as it was to think of all things they wouldn't get to do together, this was softened by recognizing everything they had already done. They were committed to seeing the world together throughout their lives instead of waiting until they were retired. Even when life was demanding and busy, and there were a million reasons not to go, they always took off time for a vacation— even if it meant a weekend of local sightseeing or cheap road tripping.

The next time you think you are too busy to take time off, ask yourself this question: a year from now will I remember the emails I answered and the meetings I attended? My guess is probably not— take the vacation and choose the memories instead.

The All-or-Nothing Pressure

The third way we put too much pressure on vacations is by believing they need to be long to be worthwhile. There genuinely are times people can't take a two-week vacation, whether because of workloads and responsibilities, caretaking duties, health factors, or because they don't have paid time off, and it isn't financially possible.

In this case, mini vacations every six to eight weeks have been shown to have tremendous benefits. Recognizing that not everyone can take a prolonged vacation, research led by University of California professor Cassie Mogilner Holmes, author of *Happier Hour*, found that you can create a positive energy boost by simply shifting your mindset and approaching a normal weekend as if it were a vacation.

Regardless of how much time off you have, there is one area where applying pressure is a good thing, and that is to put pressure on yourself to be present in whatever you are doing. Getting the most out of your time off requires being mindful with your attention to notice the positive, meaningful, funny, and memorable moments, enjoy them, and prolong them. You do this by slowing down, putting the phone away, and taking in the experience with as many senses as possible. This experience of savoring the moment, even if small and simple, is what your brain needs to ensure a memory persists, allowing you to draw on it even years later.

The Buddhist monk Bhante Gunaratana is quoted as saying, "Mindfulness gives you time. Time gives you choices. Choices skillfully made lead to freedom." And perhaps most powerful is that freedom can be found in the smallest of moments, and these noticed moments compounded over time result in a full life. As cliché as it sounds, what is the point of making a living if you never allow yourself to fully *live* the life you work so hard to create?

17

CARE in Leadership

IMAGINE you have the opportunity to interview for your ideal role. Upon arrival, the receptionist escorts you down a long hallway where you are instructed to take a seat in an empty room. You fill out some preliminary paperwork while you wait for the head of HR.

Alone in the room, you suddenly detect a strange but familiar smell. Looking around to investigate, you see white smoke coming out of a vent in the wall.

This set-up is the basis of a famous study conducted in the 1960s by psychologists John Darley and Bibb Latané. Students believed they were recruited to participate in a study on the pressures of life at an urban university, but that was just a cover. While sitting in a room filling in a questionnaire for what they thought was part of the experiment, the researchers funneled harmless white smoke through a vent. What the researchers were really interested in was how the students reacted to the smoke and if the influence of others in the room changed their reactions.

Three different conditions were tested. When students were alone in the room, within minutes of detecting the smoke, 75 percent left to report it. When three student participants who didn't know one another were in the room together, the number dropped to only 38 percent.

In a third condition, the researchers placed a single student with two "student" actors planted by the researchers. The actors were directed to respond either by ignoring the smoke altogether or acknowledging it and then pretending it was no big deal, waving it away as they continued to fill out the paperwork. In this scenario, the number of students who left the room dropped to 10 percent. The other 90 percent continued with the paperwork—as rumor has it—even as smoke impacted their ability to see and fill out the questionnaire!

It turns out that when the students were in the presence of others—especially around those who appeared unconcerned, unaffected, or seemed to be toughing it out—they were far less likely to take action, even though most would agree that smoke is indicative of a potentially dangerous situation. The social influence of others only seems to increase when those same behaviors are demonstrated by people who have (or are perceived as having) more power, authority, or information, which in this case was the planted student decoys.

In the interviews following the experiment, students shared why they didn't report the smoke. While an array of reasons was offered, what none acknowledged was how having other people in the room affected their decisions, even when this was the clearest and most significant influencer of behavior.

What might you do in this scenario? When I ask audience members, almost all share with conviction that they would be one of the 10 percent to leave the room and report the smoke. While this is an interesting study, it was also a very small one. Still, countless others like this one have shown that our decisions are more impacted by our environment and the social influence of others than we admit, predict, or are even aware of. We are social creatures, and as such, tend to follow the unspoken rules or behaviors of the social group we belong to or want to belong to. This doesn't only apply to situations that we perceive as stressful or dangerous. In a 2021 survey of more than 2,000 Britons, neuroscientist Helen Pilcher found that 67 percent admitted to laughing at jokes they didn't understand to fit in.

When thinking about this in the context of organizational culture, telling people to take breaks, set boundaries, and engage in self-care doesn't work if practicing it requires diverging from the group norm. This is especially true when taking such actions requires an element of personal vulnerability or risk. The reason is simple: doing so violates everything we've learned about our safety-seeking, self-protective, negatively biased brain. Taking breaks and practicing CARE is even less likely when leaders within an organization—whom others watch to gauge the unwritten rules and expectations of the culture—continuously sacrifice CARE practices in the name of work.

This book has focused on how we each, individually, raise our Work Vitality Quotient, regardless of title or role. After all, this is where we have the most control. Yet it is impossible to ignore the influence workplace cultures, and specifically the behaviors demonstrated by the leaders within organizations, have on our choices. If you are responsible for the work and well-being of others, or strive to be in the future, whether that be leading a team of two or an organization of thousands, there are three leadership practices that you can embody which will help create and contribute to a culture that supports vital work and people.

* Lead with empathy.

* Lead through clear expectations.

* Lead by example.

And one final note before we dive in. More people are working remotely or in hybrid work environments than ever before. This requires the development of new skills. While recognizing the need to adjust, most of the leaders I work with admit that they've found it challenging to lead well (or feel like they are doing it well) in the new world of work. You may not have the title of leader, but you can demonstrate the behaviors of leadership to influence your workplace culture. This final chapter will offer specific strategies that you can practice regardless of your title, as well as share with your leader and team to help move things in a positive direction.

Lead with Empathy

I define empathy as the ability to sense and the willingness to seek an understanding of another person's emotions, perspectives, and experiences. While undoubtedly an essential skill for leaders, especially leaders aiming to support their people in strengthening and sustaining their Work Vitality Quotient, it is a tricky behavior to demonstrate. This is because to truly engage and lead with empathy, we first need to develop it. The good news is, our brain is wired for wonder, so naturally we are designed to want to understand the world and the people we engage with. The bad news is that the busier we get, the less curious we become and the less empathetic we tend to be in our interactions with others.

At the risk of stating the obvious, to address this natural empathy shortfall, it helps to remember that the people who work for you (or anyone for that matter) are people with full lives outside of work. They are someone's partner, parent, child, friend, family member, or caretaker. Stating this isn't a judgment; but a reminder of your brain's design. As you will recall, when you are busy and stressed, your brain tends to overfocus on results and under-focus on relationships, meaning you tend to pay more attention to what you need from people versus thinking about what they need from you.

Developing an empathetic mindset starts by remembering that even if their circumstances are similar to yours, each person is unique. They face different pressures and have their own struggles. They have a life story, priorities, needs, and aspirations. Connecting to this by asking questions and showing a genuine interest in

Leaders contribute
to a workplace
culture that supports
vital people and
work when they lead
with empathy, through
clear expectations,
and by example.

---

others' lives, the challenges they face, and their overall feelings and experiences is key to leading with empathy.

While a sense of wonder helps you to develop empathy, it is demonstrated in your interactions with others. Seeing as many of your interactions in the workplace occur in meetings—particularly one-on-one meetings—these are a great place to start. While some leaders I've worked with worry that they will be perceived as intrusive if they ask personal questions, you already have a tool in your toolbox to create a safe, structured, curiosity-driven conversation—the KVI framework.

As tempting as it is to dive into details and updates, take the first five minutes of a meeting to check in with the person with whom you are meeting. To incorporate KVI check-ins, simply start off by expressing your desire to be supportive and ask, "If you are comfortable sharing, I'd like to start with an energy check-in today, specifically your levels of mental, emotional, and physical energy."

The answers shared by others can offer insights that would be impossible to observe, especially when people are working virtually. They can help reveal challenges that are keeping your people stuck in the survival zone, such as workload issues or when a lack of clarity of expectations is resulting in frustration, stress, and internal conflict. But they also create opportunities to strengthen relationships by getting to know people personally, understanding what motivates them and what doesn't, their strengths and values, and insights into how they work best from their stand-out zone. When you lead with empathy, and prioritize the person working for you instead of merely their productive output, you benefit by getting important insight into how to best support them *and* maximize their performance. But even more importantly, you demonstrate that you care about their well-being and that their success matters. As we learned during the pandemic, you don't need to be in the same building to create connection when you focus on engaging with empathy.

To further expand the application of the KVI check-in, open team meetings with them as well. You can set the stage for the check-in by simply sharing: "To help support one another so we can each do our best work in the most energizing way, let's do an energy check-in. On a scale of one to five, with five meaning you're firing on all cylinders and one, you're running on fumes, how are people feeling—mentally, emotionally, and physically?"

Given that we all work within a bigger system influenced by others, our success in that system is not achieved alone, nor should our struggles be faced alone either. In a 2022 *Harvard Business Review* article titled "Stop Framing Wellness Programs around Self-Care," the authors shared a powerful insight: "When organizations offer only individual solutions (self-care), it can send the message that employees are on their own when it comes to their mental health."

To help your team feel supported, expand the discussion to include both what people can do individually to strengthen their Work Vitality Quotient and how teams can support one another to collectively help raise one another's vitality levels. Add the following to KVI check-ins: "Is there anything you need, in the form of clarity, support, or resources, that we as a team could offer that would help you bring your best?" These conversations empower teams to see each other's well-being as a collective endeavor. Leading with an empathetic frame of mind helps to keep this front and center.

Lead through Clear Expectations
....

For the sake of clarity, I am going to be frank. While it would be unacceptable for someone to fold laundry as they sit on mute on a videoconference call during *work* time, companies rarely think twice about interrupting that same person in the evening, in the middle of their child's dance recital, or even on vacation, expecting them to sit staring at a screen in the middle of their *personal* time.

It is essential that leaders and organizations first recognize the disparity in expectations if committed to supporting employees to build more CARE into their day to generate and replenish their vitality. At a time when people are struggling to keep some semblance of separation between their work and the rest of their life, clarifying expectations will help, but clarifying *digital communication* expectations is critical. Luckily, the process of doing so can be quite straightforward.

Step one is to openly acknowledge that not all hours are business hours. Step two is to develop a team agreement about digital communication expectations. A simple template to guide the conversation includes: Identifying what methods of communication will be used, and for what purposes. Next, establish what are the response expectations for each communication method. Then, decide on agreed-upon offline times. Appreciating that emergencies will come up, identify how people will get a hold of one another in those cases. Finally, buy-in—collectively as a team, discuss the value if everyone works within the agreed-upon parameters.

Our brain's negativity bias becomes more prominent when expectations are assumed. Even if working with a very senior team or a team that has worked together for many years, setting (and resetting) communication expectations is fundamental to people being able to perform with consistency in their stand-out zone. This is especially important when starting new projects or entering times of heightened intensity. Not only does this buffer overwork and burnout, but it helps to pre-emptively intercept the emotions of fear, obligation, and guilt that often unnecessarily drive behaviors and assumptions, particularly in virtual environments. Most importantly, it creates a culture of respect and accountability.

Lead by Example

Establishing policies to help support and strengthen the Work Vitality Quotient of employees is a crucial step for organizations. However, expectations aren't just communicated in words and through policies; they are communicated through actions, and for leaders, in the examples you lead by.

"He tells me his workload is too much and is constantly challeng-ing me on priorities. I get it; everyone is working hard, and we do have too many priorities, but he has time to train for a marathon," Danica, a leader I was coaching, said. "Don't get me wrong, I'm not expecting him to work all of the time, but he obviously has the time if he really needs it."

For starters, this conversation was not occurring because Dan-ica's direct report was underperforming, in fact, the opposite was true. It was because Danica had a work-first mentality and was frus-trated her direct report did not.

The truth is that many leaders, and maybe this includes you, have been successful because of the personal sacrifices they made along the way. When work beckons, an early morning meeting gets booked, and a request comes in late on a Friday afternoon, it's a given that your free time gets sacrificed. When this happens month after month and year after year, slowly time off stops being seen as a right and starts to feel like a luxury. And intentionally or not, that becomes the example you lead by.

While taking actions that avoid or are in response to the emo-tions of fear, obligation, and guilt are strong drivers of behavior, the *reward* of feeling validated for your work-first mentality in the form of pride, approval, and applause are equally strong *and* potentially detrimental. After all, it feels good to feel successful, needed, and important. However, let's be clear, if pride, approval, and applause are driving your decisions—that is not leadership—that is *egoship*. It is your role as a leader to understand the difference as well as the ripple effect your decisions have on your team. If you don't, not only will you eventually burn yourself out, but you also risk burn-ing out your team, if not driving them away from the organization altogether. That was just what Danica was doing.

And before you go judging Danica and leaders with a similar mentality, ask yourself if you've ever responded with the old adage, "Do as I say, not as I do." There are undoubtedly many valid reasons you've said this, whether at work or in your personal life. Likely some of those reasons at work are because you are trying to protect and support your team and address the relentless demands and rising expectations you face in your own role. However, no matter how much you tell people you don't expect, or even want, them to do the same (such as check email at five-thirty in the morning), it is essential to realize that as a leader, people don't do as you say—*they do as you do*. Therefore, *you* need to do as *you* say.

How do you lead by example? It starts by remembering your actions have an outsized influence. That means as a leader, it is important to demonstrate vulnerability first, particularly when you're checking in with others or requesting they be vulnerable, by speaking to their challenges, fears, and requests for help in meetings. Share your own KVI energy check-ins, your challenges, and what you are doing to manage your energy. If you are opting to chaperone your child on a field trip instead of attending another business dinner, let people know. Share examples of when and how you have said no to a request or held a boundary. When you set your out-of-office reply, abide by it. Book your holidays in advance and take all of them. When you have a hobby or passion, share pictures and show that you can be driven in your work and live a full life outside as well.

Leading by example is how you create a work environment where people feel safe, supported, and even expected to practice CARE, ask for help, and engage in open communication when tough topics such as mental health come up. When you take actions to strengthen your Work Vitality Quotient, you lead the way for others to do the same.

It takes courage to be one of the 10 percent who notice the smoke signals and move to action—especially if others don't. Now more than ever, we need people and especially leaders to demonstrate the courage to go against the status quo, to break unhealthy group norms, and shift workplace cultures in vitality-boosting ways. Doing so doesn't just come from having the title of leader; it comes from taking leadership actions—and practicing CARE is an act of leadership.

Conclusion

JUST as I finished writing this book, a friend said to me, "You used to be such a workaholic, but you're so different now." Instead of being happy and taking it as a compliment as one might expect, I was momentarily offended. I wanted to respond and say, "Well, I still work really hard and could be a workaholic if I wanted to be!" How absolutely ridiculous! But it is also a good reminder that although a change may make logical sense, emotionally letting go of things that once served or even defined you is challenging. Admitting that I used to attach my worth to how hard I worked, and that it felt good when people noticed, feels... icky.

So, while yes, my first reaction was to resist the compliment from my friend, I said thank you. Feeling the tug of old beliefs, I reminded myself that shifting my relationship with work and my definition of success is what mattered most. Because what my friend really noticed was my renewed sense of vitality. They were experiencing the best of me when historically, they often got the leftover me. When I realized that, my friend's comment filled me with a deep, genuine joy.

Cultivating and sustaining vitality in your work is a process. Strategies, rituals, habits—these all help, but only if you are willing to *do* things differently. And that is hard, especially in toxic workplace environments that still uphold vitality-depleting beliefs and approaches. But when you are willing to shift your beliefs about success, stress, and rest, you can create a healthy, fulfilling relationship to work.

That is how you break out of the cycle of simply getting through the day—in survival mode—to reigniting your vitality to take on the day from your stand-out zone. Start by consistently practicing the small things, and then courageously experiment with the big things, and keep course correcting along the way. Your experience and relationship to work will change. But most importantly, you will change.

Acknowledgments

IS IT normal to cry the entire time you write acknowledgments? Anyone who knows me also knows I cry when I feel deep gratitude, and that is what I have for all the amazing and generous people who were a part of this book.

At the top of that list is my husband, Mike. Remember when I said this project would take six months and you suggested that I might be misjudging how big writing my first book would be? Thank you for never believing any of my time estimates and being patient when you were right. But most of all, thank you for keeping me laughing all the way through. I love you.

To my mom, we talked about this book, and you knew I could write it; I did. I miss you. To my dad, thank you for showing me you can be passionate about your work and pursue a fully lived life. I am so lucky to have grown up with you and mom as parents. Alana, my best friend and sister, where do I begin? No one heard more about this book, the research, the highs and the lows, than you. You talked with me through them all with patience, compassion, and perspective; thank you so much. This book is better, and so am I because you are my sister. Aunty, I didn't think anyone could be as proud of me as my mom, but you proved me wrong. Thank you for your love and support and text emojis to make me smile when I needed them most; Mom would be proud you finished her work getting me through this book. And while people often make jokes about their in-laws, I couldn't be luckier to have mine. Lorna, Steve, Michelle, and all of my extended family, you are the best—truly. I am so blessed to be a part of your family.

And then there is my combined cheering-challenge squad. Jasmine, Dany, Christine, Sue, Craig, Anokhee, Emily, Chris, Blair, Gemma, Mandy, Andrea, Sherry, Natalia, David, Claire, Linda, Judi (and many others who helped in different ways), you each pushed, prodded, and propelled me forward at different times in my life and with different types of support, from the inception of the ideas to the moment I hit send on the final manuscript—thank you so much. Your fingerprints are all over this. To my ladies, Sarah, Nicole, and Shannon, even when you had no idea what I was writing about, you cheered me on anyway. Everyone needs friends like you. Lorie, the evenings sitting in the backyard talking through these ideas and your vulnerability helped me think differently and more deeply; thank you.

To Jennie Nash, my book proposal coach. You have made me better in more ways than I can ever explain; thank you for not letting me write the easy book and pushing me to write this one. You helped me shape these ideas. And Kendra Ward, my magic-maker editor. I have never felt so supported and encouraged. You found a way to identify the elements that made everything better. To my project manager, Adrineh, thank you for always being so kind in your efforts to keep me on track—not an easy task! I hope I didn't drive either of you crazy, because I feel you're both too kind to tell me if I did. To everyone else at Page Two, with special thanks to Jesse Finkelstein. I had my eye on you as a female-owned and -operated publisher, and working with you and all of the team at Page Two has been better than I could have imagined. Thank you for seeing the possibilities in this project and taking me on and pushing me through.

Jeanette, Donna, and everyone at Powell Speakers, I can't begin to express my gratitude. Not only do I love you all, but you believed in me and protected my schedule at times to help me get this done. If hugs could come through a page, know I am giving you all one now.

To Brittanny Kreutzer, Don Jenkins, Richard Schelp, Tim Mathy, and all of your colleagues at your respective bureaus. You were the first agents who believed in me and gave me the opportunity to work with your clients when I started speaking. You are all legends, and I am deeply grateful for your support and guidance. A special shout-out to Brittanny and Novozymes, together you gave me the first chance to share these ideas and over the years of researching it to test and sharpen the concepts. Thank you—this book grew out of that first opportunity.

My family at IHHP. I cut my teeth with you and I learned so much in my time working with you and all of our amazing clients. You all will hold a special place in my heart. Cranla, thank you for living by the philosophy that it's better to ask for forgiveness than permission (wink). You are such a key person behind why I am doing what I love today; thank you.

While we are not friends (yet), I need to thank three incredible women whose work has had an indelible impact on me. Kelly McGonigal for your book *The Upside of Stress*. I don't say this lightly, but that book changed my life and my work. To Arianna Huffington, you are a legend leading the way with Thrive Global toward a world that celebrates and supports thriving as a success outcome instead of burnout. I hope this work contributes to that mission because your work has contributed to mine. And finally, to Jen Fisher, chief well-being officer at Deloitte. You are DOING the work; you are proving that even in one of the most esteemed organizations, well-being and life-work integration are not only possible, but they are also being done. Your humility, expertise, and dedication to giving organizations and their people the tools to build healthy, human-centered cultures is a model I work toward as well. Thank you for leading the way.

To the clients who trusted me, the audiences who challenged me, the research participants who allowed me to learn, and the nameless people who sat beside me on planes and everywhere else this book's ideas were explored and tested—thank you.

Finally, to humans. Thank you for letting me observe you. You are confusing, angering, and beautiful, and because of you, I feel alive doing the work I do.

Bibliography

Chapter 1: Your Work Vitality Quotient

de Jonge, Jan, and Maria C.W. Peeters. "The Vital Worker: Towards Sustainable Performance at Work." *International Journal of Environmental Research and Public Health* vol. 16, no. 6 (2019). doi.org/10.3390/ijerph16060910.

Goldsmith, Marshall. "Improve Your Leadership with Six Simple Daily Questions." Duke Corporate Education, December 2016. dukece.com/insights/improve-leadership-six-simple-daily-questions/.

Huffington, Arianna. "Is Success without Well-Being Really Success?" *The SHRM Blog*, March 22, 2022. blog.shrm.org/blog/is-success-without-well-being-really-success.

Lavrusheva, Olga. "The Concept of Vitality: Review of the Vitality-Related Research Domain." *New Ideas in Psychology* vol. 56 (2020). doi.org/10.1016/j.newideapsych.2019.100752.

Lund, Susan, et al. *The Future of Work after COVID-19*. McKinsey & Company, February 18, 2021. mckinsey.com/featured-insights/future-of-work/the-future-of-work-after-covid-19.

Napper, Paul, and Anthony Rao. "How to Develop Your Sense of Agency." *Mindful*, April 15, 2019. mindful.org/seven-ways-to-develop-personal-agency.

Ryan, Richard M., and Christina Frederick. "On Energy, Personality, and Health: Subjective Vitality as a Dynamic Reflection of Well-Being." *Journal of Personality* vol. 65, no. 3 (1997): 529–65. doi.org/10.1111/j.1467-6494.1997.tb00326.x.

Ryan, Richard M., and Edward L. Deci. "From Ego Depletion to Vitality: Theory and Findings Concerning the Facilitation of Energy Available to the Self." *Social and Personality Psychology Compass* vol. 2, no. 2 (2008): 702–17. doi.org/10.1111/j.1751-9004.2008.00098.x.

University of Sussex. "Meaningful Work Not Created, Only Destroyed, by Bosses, Study Finds." *ScienceDaily*, June 3, 2016. sciencedaily.com/releases/2016/06/160603110259.htm.

Wörtler, Burkhard, et al. "The Link between Employees' Sense of Vitality and Proactivity: Investigating the Moderating Role of Personal Fear of Invalidity." *Frontiers in Psychology* vol. 11 (2020). doi.org/10.3389/fpsyg.2020.02169.

Chapter 2: The Science of Your Work Vitality

Arnsten, Amy F.T., et al. "The Effects of Stress Exposure on Prefrontal Cortex: Translating Basic Research Into Successful Treatments for Post-traumatic Stress Disorder." *Neurobiology of Stress* vol. 1 (2015): 89–99. doi.org/10.1016/j.ynstr.2014.10.002.

Berkovic, Eva. "Why Does Your Brain Love Negativity? The Negativity Bias." Marbella International University Centre, February 8, 2017. miuc.org/brain-love-negativity-negativity-bias.

Bonnet, Louise, et al. "The Role of the Amygdala in the Perception of Positive Emotions: An 'Intensity Detector.'" *Behavioral Neuroscience* vol. 9 (2015). doi.org/10.3389/fnbeh.2015.00178.

Cable, Daniel M. *Alive at Work: The Neuroscience of Helping Your People Love What They Do*. Boston: Harvard Business Review Press, 2019.

Charles, Susan T., et al. "The Wear and Tear of Daily Stressors on Mental Health." *Psychological Science* vol. 24, no. 5 (2013): 733–41. doi.org/10.1177/0956797612462222.

Deci, Edward L., and Richard M. Ryan. "The 'What' and 'Why' of Goal Pursuits: Human Needs and the Self-Determination of Behavior." *Psychological Inquiry* vol. 11, no. 4 (2000): 227–68. doi.org/10.1207/S15327965PLI1104_01.

Godoy, Lívea Dornela, et al. "A Comprehensive Overview on Stress Neurobiology: Basic Concepts and Clinical Implications." *Frontiers in Behavioral Neuroscience* vol. 12 (2018). doi.org/10.3389/fnbeh.2018.00127.

Guidi, Jenny, et al. "Allostatic Load and Its Impact on Health: A Systematic Review." *Psychotherapy and Psychosomatics* vol. 90 (2020): 11–27. doi.org/10.1159/000510696.

Kashdan, Todd B. "Wired to Wonder." *Greater Good Magazine*, September 1, 2009. greatergood.berkeley.edu/article/item/wired_to_wonder.

McEwen, Bruce S. "Protective and Damaging Effects of Stress Mediators: Central Role of the Brain." *Dialogues in Clinical Neuroscience* vol. 8, no. 4 (2006): 367–81. doi.org/10.31887/DCNS.2006.8.4/bmcewen.

Ryan, Richard M., and Edward L. Deci. "Self-Determination Theory and the Facilitation of Intrinsic Motivation, Social Development, and Well-Being." *American Psychologist* vol. 55, no. 1 (2000): 68–78. doi.org/10.1037/0003-066X.55.1.68.

Salzman, C. Daniel. "Amygdala." *Encyclopedia Britannica*, updated September 8, 2022. britannica.com/science/amygdala.

Vaish, Amrisha, et al. "Not All Emotions Are Created Equal: The Negativity Bias in Social-Emotional Development." *Psychological Bulletin* vol. 134, no. 3 (2008): 383–403. doi.org/10.1037/0033-2909.134.3.383.

Chapter 3: Establishing Your Key Vitality Indicators

Fatigue Science. *The Science of Sleep*. Vancouver, BC: Fatigue Science, 2018. fatiguescience.com/wp-content/uploads/2018/02/Fatigue-Science-Science-of-Sleep-eBook.pdf.

Van Dongen, Hans P.A., et al. "The Cumulative Cost of Additional Wakefulness: Dose-Response Effects on Neurobehavioral Functions and Sleep Physiology from Chronic Sleep Restriction and Total Sleep Deprivation." *Sleep* vol. 26, no. 2 (2003): 117–26. doi.org/10.1093/sleep/26.2.117.

Chapter 4: The Success Traps

Brosi, Prisca, and Fabiola H. Gerpott. "Stayed at Home—But Can't Stop Working despite Being Ill?! Guilt as a Driver of Presenteeism at Work and Home." *Journal of Organizational Behavior* (2022). doi.org/10.1002/job.2601.

Chapter 5: The Trap of Believing You're Burnout Proof

Kim, Jae Yun, et al. "Understanding Contemporary Forms of Exploitation: Attributions of Passion Serve to Legitimize the Poor Treatment of Workers." *Journal of Personality and Social Psychology* vol. 118, no. 1 (2020): 121–48. doi.org/10.1037/pspi0000190.

Moeller, Julia, et al. "Highly Engaged but Burned Out: Intra-individual Profiles in the US Workforce." *Career Development International* vol. 23, no. 1 (2018): 86–105. doi.org/10.1108/CDI-12-2016-0215.

Chapter 6: The Trap of Always Being Available

Shah, J., and E.T. Higgins. "Expectancy × Value Effects: Regulatory Focus as Determinant of Magnitude *and* Direction." *Journal of Personality and Social Psychology* vol. 73, no. 3 (1997): 447–58. doi.org/10.1037/0022-3514.73.3.447.

Chapter 7: The Trap of Equating More Hours with Advantage

Amabile, Teresa, and Steven Kramer. *The Progress Principle: Using Small Wins to Ignite Joy, Engagement, and Creativity at Work*. Cambridge: Harvard Business Review Press, 2011.

Buehler, Roger, et al. "The Planning Fallacy: Cognitive, Motivational, and
    Social Origins." *Advances in Experimental Social Psychology* vol. 43 (2010):
    1–62. doi.org/10.1016/S0065-2601(10)43001-4.

Fitch, John, and Max Frenzel. *Time Off: A Practical Guide to Building Your Rest
    Ethic and Finding Success without the Stress*. Illustrated by Mariya Suzuki.
    Austin, TX: Time Off LLC, 2020.

Gilbert, Daniel T., and Jane E. Ebert. "Decisions and Revisions: The Affective
    Forecasting of Changeable Outcomes." *Journal of Personality
    and Social Psychology* vol. 82, no. 4 (2002): 503–14. doi.org/10.1037/
    0022-3514.82.4.503.

Chapter 8: The Trap of the Highest Standards

Batts Allen, Ashley, and Mark R. Leary. "Self-Compassion, Stress, and
    Coping." *Social and Personality Psychology Compass* vol. 4, no. 2 (2010):
    107–118. doi.org/10.1111/j.1751-9004.2009.00246.x.

Kotera, Yasuhiro, and William Van Gordon. "Effects of Self-Compassion
    Training on Work-Related Well-Being: A Systematic Review." *Frontiers
    in Psychology* vol. 12 (2021). doi.org/10.3389/fpsyg.2021.630798.

Longe, Olivia, et al. "Having a Word with Yourself: Neural Correlates of
    Self-Criticism and Self-Reassurance." *Neuroimage* vol. 49, no. 2 (2010):
    1849–56. doi.org/10.1016/j.neuroimage.2009.09.019.

Luo, Xi, Lei Qiao, and Xianwei Che. "Self-Compassion Modulates Heart Rate
    Variability and Negative Affect to Experimentally Induced Stress."
    Mindfulness vol. 9 (2018): 1522–28. doi.org/10.1007/s12671-018-0900-9.

Neff, Kristin. "Definition of Self-Compassion." *Self-Compassion*,
    self-compassion.org/the-three-elements-of-self-compassion-2.

Neff, Kristin. "The Five Myths of Self-Compassion." *Greater Good Magazine*,
    September 30, 2015. greatergood.berkeley.edu/article/item/
    the_five_myths_of_self_compassion.

Neff, Kristin D., Ya-Ping Hsieh, and Kullaya Dejitterat. "Self-Compassion,
    Achievement Goals, and Coping with Academic Failure." *Self and Identity*
    vol. 4, no. 3 (2005): 263–87. doi.org/10.1080/13576500444000317.

Swider, Brian, et al. "The Pros and Cons of Perfectionism, According to
    Research." *Harvard Business Review*, December 27, 2018. hbr.org/2018/12/
    the-pros-and-cons-of-perfectionism-according-to-research.

Chapter 9: Getting Better at Stress

Brewer, Judson. *Unwinding Anxiety: New Science Shows How to Break the
    Cycles of Worry and Fear to Heal Your Mind*. New York: Avery Publishing
    Group, 2021.

Charles, Susan T., et al. "The Wear and Tear of Daily Stressors on
  Mental Health." *Psychological Science* vol. 24, no. 5 (2013): 733–41.
  doi.org/10.1177/0956797612462222.

Chiu, Allyson. "Time to Ditch 'Toxic Positivity,' Experts Say: 'It's Okay
  Not to Be Okay.'" *Washington Post*, August 19, 2020. washingtonpost.com/
  lifestyle/wellness/toxic-positivity-mental-health-covid/2020/08/19/
  5dff8d16-e0c8-11ea-8181-606e603bb1c4_story.html.

David, Susan. *Emotional Agility: Get Unstuck, Embrace Change, and Thrive in
  Work and Life*. New York: Avery Publishing Group, 2016.

Goleman, Daniel. *Emotional Intelligence: Why It Can Matter More Than IQ*.
  London: Bloomsbury Publishing, 1995.

Hamilton, Diane Musho. "Calming Your Brain during Conflict." *Harvard
  Business Review*, December 22, 2015. hbr.org/2015/12/calming-your-brain-
  during-conflict.

Hutmacher, Fabian. "Putting Stress in Historical Context: Why It Is Important
  That Being Stressed Out Was Not a Way to Be a Person 2,000 Years Ago."
  Frontiers in Psychology vol. 12 (2021). doi.org/10.3389/fpsyg.2021.539799.

Kreider, Tim. "The 'Busy' Trap." *New York Times*, June 30, 2012.
  opinionator.blogs.nytimes.com/2012/06/30/the-busy-trap.

Lieberman, Charlotte. "Why You Procrastinate (It Has Nothing to Do with
  Self-Control)." *New York Times*, March 25, 2019. nytimes.com/2019/03/25/
  smarter-living/why-you-procrastinate-it-has-nothing-to-do-with-self-
  control.html.

McGonigal, Kelly. *The Upside of Stress: Why Stress Is Good for You, and How to
  Get Good at It*. New York: Avery Publishing Group, 2016.

Parker, Clifton P. "Embracing Stress Is More Important Than Reducing
  Stress, Stanford Psychologist Says." *Stanford News*, May 7, 2015.
  news.stanford.edu/2015/05/07/stress-embrace-mcgonigal-050715/.

Semnani, Neda. "A Harvard Psychologist Explains Why Forcing Positive
  Thinking Won't Make You Happy." *Washington Post*, September 23, 2016.
  washingtonpost.com/news/inspired-life/wp/2016/09/23/forcing-positive-
  thinking-wont-make-you-happy-says-this-harvard-psychologist/.

Sirois, Fuschia, and Timothy Pychyl. "Procrastination and the Priority of
  Short-Term Mood Regulation: Consequences for Future Self." *Social and
  Personality Psychology Compass* vol. 7, no. 2 (2013): 115–27. doi.org/10.1111/
  spc3.12011.

University of Texas at Austin. "Psychologists Find the Meaning of Aggression:
  'Monty Python' Scene Helps Research." *ScienceDaily*, March 24, 2011.
  sciencedaily.com/releases/2011/03/110323105202.htm.

Viviani, Roberto, et al. "Signals of Anticipation of Reward and of Mean Reward
  Rates in the Human Brain." *Scientific Reports* vol. 10 (2020). doi.org/10.1038/
  s41598-020-61257-y.

Wigert, Ben, and Sangeeta Agrawal. "Employee Burnout, Part 1: The 5 Main Causes." Gallup Workplace, July 12, 2018. gallup.com/workplace/237059/employee-burnout-part-main-causes.aspx.

Chapter 10: Using a "Yes, and" Stress Mindset

Brooks, Alison Wood. "Get Excited: Reappraising Pre-performance Anxiety as Excitement." *Journal of Experimental Psychology: General* vol. 143, no. 3 (2014): 1144–58. doi.org/10.1037/a0035325.

Crum, Alia J., Peter Salovey, and Shawn Achor. "Rethinking Stress: The Role of Mindsets in Determining the Stress Response." *Journal of Personality and Social Psychology* vol. 104, no. 4 (2013): 716–33. doi.org/10.1037/a0031201.

Crum, Alia J., et al. "The Role of Stress Mindset in Shaping Cognitive, Emotional, and Physiological Responses to Challenging and Threatening Stress." *Anxiety, Stress, & Coping* vol. 30, no. 4 (2017): 379–95. doi.org/10.1080/10615806.2016.1275585.

Epel, Elissa S., Bruce S. McEwen, and Jeannette R. Ickovics. "Embodying Psychological Thriving: Physical Thriving in Response to Stress." *Journal of Social Issues* vol. 54, no. 2 (1998), 301–22. doi.org/10.1111/0022-4537.671998067.

Howes, Lewis. "Psychologist Explains the Secret to Making Stress Your Friend | Kelly McGonigal & Lewis Howes." *School of Greatness* podcast, YouTube, September 14, 2020. youtube.com/watch?v=ZY5Ck3qU3eY&t=275s.

Hutmacher, Fabian. "Putting Stress in Historical Context: Why It Is Important That Being Stressed Out Was Not a Way to Be a Person 2,000 Years Ago." *Frontiers in Psychology* vol. 12 (2021). doi.org/10.3389/fpsyg.2021.539799.

Jamieson, Jeremy P., et al. "Mind over Matter: Reappraising Arousal Improves Cardiovascular and Cognitive Responses to Stress." *Journal of Experimental Psychology: General* vol. 141, no. 3 (2012): 417–22. doi.org/10.1037/a0025719.

Jamieson, Jeremy P., et al. "Optimizing Stress Responses with Reappraisal and Mindset Interventions: An Integrated Model." *Anxiety, Stress, & Coping* vol. 31, no. 3 (2018): 245–61, doi.org/10.1080/10615806.2018.1442615.

Jamieson, Jeremy P., Wendy Berry Mendes, and Matthew K. Nock. "Improving Acute Stress Responses: The Power of Reappraisal." *Current Directions in Psychological Science* vol. 22, no. 1 (2013): 51–56. doiorg/10.1177/0963721412461500.

Kassam, Karim S., Katrina Koslov, and Wendy Berry Mendes. "Decisions under Distress: Stress Profiles Influence Anchoring and Adjustment." *Psychological Science* vol. 20, no. 11 (2009): 1394–99. doi.org/10.1111/j.1467-9280.2009.02455.x.

McGonigal, Kelly. *The Upside of Stress: Why Stress Is Good for You, and How to Get Good at It.* New York: Avery Publishing Group, 2016.

Robertson, Ian. "How Freaking Out Can Help You Succeed, According to Science." *Time*, January 3, 2017. time.com/4592069/stress-stronger-science/.

Selna, Elaine. "How Some Stress Can Actually Be Good for You." *Time*, November 20, 2018. time.com/5434826/stress-good-health.

Smith, Eric N., Michael D. Young, and Alia J. Crum. "Stress, Mindsets, and Success in Navy SEALs Special Warfare Training." *Frontiers in Psychology* vol. 10 (2020). doi.org/10.3389/fpsyg.2019.02962.

Tedeschi, Richard G., and Lawrence G. Calhoun. "Posttraumatic Growth: Conceptual Foundations and Empirical Evidence," *Psychological Inquiry* vol. 15, no. 1 (2004): 1–18. doi.org/10.1207/s15327965pli1501_01.

Chapter 11: Transforming Your Stress Response

Goldberg, Haley. "Your Attitude about Aging Could Add 7.5 Years to Your Life." *New York Post*, April 23, 2022. nypost.com/2022/04/23/your-bad-attitude-about-aging-could-add-7-5-years-to-your-life.

Grossmann, Igor, Harrison Oakes, and Henri C. Santos. "Wise Reasoning Benefits from Emodiversity, Irrespective of Emotional Intensity." *Journal of Experimental Psychology* vol. 148, no. 5 (2019): 805–23. doi.org/10.1037/xge0000543.

Lieberman, Matthew D., et al. "Putting Feelings Into Words: Affect Labeling Disrupts Amygdala Activity in Response to Affective Stimuli." *Psychological Science* vol. 18, no. 5 (2007): 421–28. doi.org/10.1111/j.1467-9280.2007.01916.x.

Ong, Anthony D., et al. "Emodiversity and Biomarkers of Inflammation." *Emotion* vol. 18, no. 1 (2018): 3–14. doi.org/10.1037/emo0000343.

Chapter 12: Keeping Small Stress Small

Aldwin, Carolyn M., et al. "Do Hassles Mediate between Life Events and Mortality in Older Men? Longitudinal Findings from the VA Normative Aging Study." *Experimental Gerontology* vol. 59 (2014): 74–80. doi.org/10.1016/j.exger.2014.06.019.

Mead, Nicole L. "Simple Pleasures, Small Annoyances, and Goal Progress in Daily Life." *Journal of the Association for Consumer Research* vol. 1, no. 4 (2016). doi.org/10.1086/688287.

Oregon State University. "Even Small Stressors May Be Harmful to Men's Health, New OSU Research Shows." OSU Newsroom, September 10, 2014. today.oregonstate.edu/archives/2014/sep/even-small-stressors-may-be-harmful-men's-health-new-osu-research-shows.

Piazza, Jennifer R., et al. "Affective Reactivity to Daily Stressors and Long-Term Risk of Reporting a Chronic Physical Health Condition." *Annals of Behavioral Medicine* vol. 45, no. 1 (2013): 110–20. doi.org/10.1007/s12160-012-9423-0.

Chapter 13: Re-energizing You

Aryanti, Ratih Devi, Erita Diah Sari, and Herlina Siwi Widiana. "A Literature Review of Workplace Well-Being." *Advances in Social Science, Education and Humanities Research* vol. 477 (2020). doi.org/10.2991/assehr.k.201017.134.

Grant, Adam. "There's a Name for the Blah You're Feeling: It's Called Languishing." *New York Times*, April 19, 2021. nytimes.com/2021/04/19/well/mind/covid-mental-health-languishing.html.

Keyes, Corey L.M. "The Mental Health Continuum: From Languishing to Flourishing in Life." *Journal of Health and Social Behavior* vol. 43, no. 2 (2002): 207–22. doi.org/10.2307/3090197.

Martínez, Nicole, et al. "Self-Care: A Concept Analysis." *International Journal of Nursing Sciences* vol. 8, no. 4 (2021): 418–25, doi.org/10.1016/j.ijnss.2021.08.007.

Monroe, Chelsie, et al. "The Value of Intentional Self-Care Practices: The Effects of Mindfulness on Improving Job Satisfaction, Teamwork, and Workplace Environments." *Archives of Psychiatric Nursing* vol. 35, no. 2 (2021): 189–94. doi.org/10.1016/j.apnu.2020.10.003.

Posluns, Kirsten, and Terry Lynn Gall. "Dear Mental Health Practitioners, Take Care of Yourselves: A Literature Review on Self-Care." *International Journal for the Advancement of Counselling* vol. 42, no. 1 (2020): 1–20. doi.org/10.1007/s10447-019-09382-w.

Weziak-Bialowolska, Dorota, et al. "Well-Being in Life and Well-Being at Work: Which Comes First? Evidence from a Longitudinal Study." *Frontiers in Public Health* vol. 8 (2020). doi.org/10.3389/fpubh.2020.00103.

Chapter 14: The CARE Index

Bethelmy, Lisbeth C., and José A. Corraliza. "Transcendence and Sublime Experience in Nature: Awe and Inspiring Energy." *Frontiers in Psychology* vol. 10 (2019). doi.org/10.3389/fpsyg.2019.00509.

Coulson, Jo C., Jim McKenna, and M. Field. "Exercising at Work and Self-Reported Work Performance." *International Journal of Workplace Health Management* vol. 1, no. 3 (2008): 176–97. doi.org/10.1108/17538350810926534.

Desai, Shreya, et al. "A Systematic Review and Meta-analysis on the Effects of Exercise on the Endocannabinoid System." *Cannabis and Cannabinoid Research* vol. 7, no. 4 (2022). doi.org/10.1089/can.2021.0113.

Di Stefano, Giada, et al. "Making Experience Count: The Role of Reflection in Individual Learning." Harvard Business School Working Paper No. 14-093 (2014). doi.org/10.2139/ssrn.2414478.

Eschleman, Kevin J., et al. "Benefiting from Creative Activity: The Positive Relationships between Creative Activity, Recovery Experiences, and Performance-Related Outcomes." *Journal of Occupational and Organizational Psychology* vol. 87, no. 3 (2014): 579–98. doi.org/10.1111/joop.12064.

Fancourt, Daisy, Simon Opher, and Cesar de Oliveira. "Fixed-Effects Analyses of Time-Varying Associations between Hobbies and Depression in a Longitudinal Cohort Study: Support for Social Prescribing?" *Psychotherapy and Psychosomatics* vol. 89, no. 2 (2020): 111–13. doi.org/10.1159/000503571.

Hasan, Hunaid, and Tasneem Fatema Hasan. "Laugh Yourself into a Healthier Person: A Cross Cultural Analysis of the Effects of Varying Levels of Laughter on Health." *International Journal of Medical Sciences* vol. 6, no. 4 (2009): 200–11. doi.org/10.7150/ijms.6.200.

Heissel, Jennifer A., Dorainne J. Levy, and Emma K. Adam. "Stress, Sleep, and Performance on Standardized Tests: Understudied Pathways to the Achievement Gap." *AERA Open* vol. 3, no. 3 (2017). doi.org/10.1177/2332858417713488.

Hirotsu, Camila, Sergio Tufik, and Monica Levy Andersen. "Interactions between Sleep, Stress, and Metabolism: From Physiological to Pathological Conditions." *Sleep Science* vol. 8, no. 3 (2013): 143–52. doi.org/10.1016/j.slsci.2015.09.002.

Hu, Hai-hua, et al. "Strong Ties versus Weak Ties in Word-of-Mouth Marketing." *BRQ Business Research Quarterly* vol. 22, no. 4 (2019): 245–56. doi.org/10.1016/j.brq.2018.10.004.

Keng, Shian-Ling, Moria J. Smoski, and Clive J. Robins. "Effects of Mindfulness on Psychological Health: A Review of Empirical Studies." *Clinical Psychology Review* vol. 31, no. 6 (2011): 1041–56. doi.org/10.1016/j.cpr.2011.04.006.

Klaperski, Sandra, et al. "Optimizing Mental Health Benefits of Exercise: The Influence of the Exercise Environment on Acute Stress Levels and Wellbeing." *Mental Health & Prevention* vol. 15 (2019). doi.org/10.1016/j.mhp.2019.200173.

Laursen, Lucas, and Kurt Kleiner. "Illusions of Steepness and Height." *SA Mind* vol. 19, no. 5 (2008). doi.org/10.1038/scientificamericanmind1008-12.

Liu, Patrick Z., and Robin Nusslock. "Exercise-Mediated Neurogenesis in the Hippocampus via BDNF." *Frontiers in Neuroscience* vol. 12, no. 52 (2018). doi.org/10.3389/fnins.2018.00052.

Mandolesi, Laura, et al. "Effects of Physical Exercise on Cognitive Functioning and Wellbeing: Biological and Psychological Benefits." *Frontiers in Psychology* vol. 9 (2018). doi.org/10.3389/fpsyg.2018.00509.

Marusak, Hilary A. "The 'Runner's High' May Result from Molecules Called Cannabinoids—The Body's Own Version of THC and CBD." *The Conversation*, December 17, 2021. theconversation.com/the-runners-high-may-result-from-molecules-called-cannabinoids-the-bodys-own-version-of-thc-and-cbd-170796.

Mull, Amanda. "The Pandemic Has Erased Entire Categories of Friendship." *The Atlantic*, January 27, 2021. theatlantic.com/health/archive/2021/01/pandemic-goodbye-casual-friends/617839/.

Piccirillo, Rosanna. "Exercise-Induced Myokines with Therapeutic Potential for Muscle Wasting." *Frontiers in Physiology* vol. 10 (2019). doi.org/10.3389/fphys.2019.00287.

Prinzing, Michael M., et al. "Staying 'in Sync' with Others during COVID-19: Perceived Positivity Resonance Mediates Cross-Sectional and Longitudinal Links between Trait Resilience and Mental Health." *Journal of Positive Psychology* vol. 17, no. 3 (2022): 440–55. doi.org/10.1080/17439760.2020.1858336.

Ryan, Richard M., et al. "Vitalizing Effects of Being Outdoors and in Nature." *Journal of Environmental Psychology* vol. 30, no. 2 (2010): 159–68. doi.org/10.1016/j.jenvp.2009.10.009.

Saghir, Zahid, et al. "The Amygdala, Sleep Debt, Sleep Deprivation, and the Emotion of Anger: A Possible Connection?" *Cureus* vol. 10, no. 7 (2018). doi.org/10.7759/cureus.2912.

Schnall, Simone, et al. "Social Support and the Perception of Geographical Slant." *Journal of Experimental Social Psychology* vol. 44, no. 5 (2008): 1246–55. doi.org/10.1016/j.jesp.2008.04.011.

Seppälä, Emma, and Marissa King. "Burnout at Work Isn't Just about Exhaustion. It's Also about Loneliness." *Harvard Business Review*, June 29, 2017. hbr.org/2017/06burnout-at-work-isnt-just-about-exhaustion-its-also-about-loneliness.

Sleiman, Sama F., et al. "Exercise Promotes the Expression of Brain Derived Neurotrophic Factor (BDNF) through the Action of the Ketone Body-Hydroxybutyrate." *eLife* vol. 5 (2016). doi.org/10.7554/eLife.15092.

Suttie, Jill. "Five Ways Mindfulness Meditation Is Good for Your Health." *Greater Good Magazine*, October 24, 2018. greatergood.berkeley.edu/article/item/five_ways_mindfulness_meditation_is_good_for_your_health.

Ulrich, Roger S. "View through a Window May Influence Recovery from Surgery." *Science* vol. 224, no. 4647 (1984): 420–21. doi.org/10.1126/science.6143402.

van den Berg, Magdalena, et al. "Visiting Green Space Is Associated with Mental Health and Vitality: A Cross-Sectional Study in Four European Cities." *Health & Place* no. 38 (2016): 8–15. doi.org/10.1016/j.healthplace.2016.01.003.

Zomorodi, Manoush. "Matthew Walker: Why Is It Essential to Make Time for Sleep?" *TED Radio Hour*, NPR, February 5, 2021. npr.org/transcripts/964209001.

Chapter 15: CARE at Work

André, Christophe. "Proper Breathing Brings Better Health." *Scientific American*, January 15, 2019. scientificamerican.com/article/proper-breathing-brings-better-health/.

Bergouignan, Audrey, et al. "Effect of Frequent Interruptions of Prolonged Sitting on Self-Perceived Levels of Energy, Mood, Food Cravings and Cognitive Function." *International Journal of Behavioral Nutrition and Physical Activity* vol. 13, no. 1 (2016). doi.org/10.1186/s12966-016-0437-z.

Dababneh, Awwad J., Naomi Swanson, and Richard L. Shell. "Impact of Added Rest Breaks on the Productivity and Well Being of Workers." *Ergonomics* vol. 44, no. 2 (2001): 164–74. doi.org/10.1080/00140130121538.

Doodle. "The Time Blocking Report." Accessed May 12, 2022. doodle.com/fr/resources/research-and-reports/time-blocking-report.

Dorion, Dominique, and Simon Darveau. "Do Micropauses Prevent Surgeon's Fatigue and Loss of Accuracy Associated with Prolonged Surgery? An Experimental Prospective Study." *Annals of Surgery* vol. 257, no. 2 (2013): 256–59. doi.org/10.1097/SLA.0b013e31825efe87.

Herrero, Jose L., et al. "Breathing above the Brain Stem: Volitional Control and Attentional Modulation in Humans." *Journal of Neurophysiology* vol. 119, no. 1 (2018): 145–59. doi.org/10.1152/jn.00551.2017.

Kim, Sooyeol, Seonghee Cho, and YoungAh Park. "Daily Microbreaks in a Self-Regulatory Resources Lens: Perceived Health Climate as a Contextual Moderator via Microbreak Autonomy." *Journal of Applied Psychology* vol. 107, no. 1 (2022): 60–77. doi.org/10.1037/apl0000891.

Lu, Jackson G., Modupe Akinola, and Malia F. Mason. "'Switching On' Creativity: Task Switching Can Increase Creativity by Reducing Cognitive Fixation." *Organizational Behavior and Human Decision Processes* vol. 139 (2017): 63–75. doi.org/10.1016/j.obhdp.2017.01.005.

Lundberg, John O.N., et al. "Inhalation of Nasally Derived Nitric Oxide Modulates Pulmonary Function in Humans." *Acta Physiologica Scandinavica* vol. 158, no. 4 (1996): 343–47. doi.org/10.1046/j.1365-201X.1996.557321000.x.

Lupu, Ioana, Mayra Ruiz-Castro, and Bernard Leca. "Role Distancing and the Persistence of Long Work Hours in Professional Service Firms." *Organization Studies* vol. 43, no. 1 (2022). doi.org/10.1177/0170840620934064.

O'Dolan, Catriona, et al. "A Randomised Feasibility Study to Investigate the Impact of Education and the Addition of Prompts on the Sedentary Behaviour of Office Workers." *Pilot and Feasibility Studies* vol. 4 (2018). doi.org/10.1186/s40814-017-0226-8.

Pickard-Whitehead, Gabrielle. "Schedule Breaks from Work? There's a Good Chance You Get Interrupted Anyway." *Small Business Trends*, May 25, 2021. smallbiztrends.com/2021/05/scheduled-breaks-getting-interrupted.html.

Scholz, André, et al. "Methods in Experimental Work Break Research: A Scoping Review." *International Journal of Environmental Research and Public Health* vol. 16, no. 20 (2019). doi.org/10.3390/ijerph16203844.

Schulte, Brigid. "Preventing Busyness from Becoming Burnout." *Harvard Business Review*, April 15, 2019. hbr.org/2019/04/preventing-busyness-from-becoming-burnout.

Stone, Linda. "Just Breathe: Building the Case for Email Apnea." *Huffington Post*, February 8, 2008. huffpost.com/entry/just-breathe-building-the_b_85651.

University of Illinois at Urbana-Champaign. "Brief Diversions Vastly Improve Focus, Researchers Find." *ScienceDaily*, February 8, 2011. sciencedaily.com/releases/2011/02/110208131529.htm.

Chapter 16: CARE Away from Work

Broadway, James M., and Brittiney Sandoval. "Why Does Time Seem to Speed Up with Age?" *SA Mind* vol. 27, no. 4 (2016). doi.org/10.1038/scientificamericanmind0716-73.

Casper, Anne, Sabine Sonnentag, and Stephanie Tremmel. "Mindset Matters: The Role of Employees' Stress Mindset for Day-Specific Reactions to Workload Anticipation." *European Journal of Work & Organizational Psychology* vol. 26, no. 6 (2017): 798–810. doi.org/10.1080/1359432X.2017.1374947.

Duszkiewicz, Adrian J., et al. "Novelty and Dopaminergic Modulation of Memory Persistence: A Tale of Two Systems." *Trends in Neurosciences* vol. 42, no. 2 (2019): 102–14. doi.org/10.1016/J.TINS.2018.10.002.

Mogilner Holmes, Cassie. "Treat Your Weekend like a Vacation." *Harvard Business Review*, January 31, 2019. hbr.org/2019/01/treat-your-weekend-like-a-vacation.

Pang, Alex Soojung-Kim. "The Secrets to a Truly Restorative Vacation." ideas.ted.com, December 20, 2016. ideas.ted.com/the-secrets-to-a-truly-restorative-vacation.

Pedersen, Walker S., et al. "The Effects of Stimulus Novelty and Negativity on BOLD Activity in the Amygdala, Hippocampus, and Bed Nucleus of the Stria Terminalis." *Social Cognitive and Affective Neuroscience* vol. 12, no. 5 (2017): 748–57. doi.org/10.1093/scan/nsw178.

TED. "Why Our Screens Make Us Less Happy | Adam Alter." TED talk (Vancouver, BC), YouTube, April 2017. youtube.com/watch?v=0K5OO2ybueM.

Tonietto, Gabriela N., et al. "Viewing Leisure as Wasteful Undermines Enjoyment." *Journal of Experimental Social Psychology* vol. 97 (2021). doi.org/10.1016/j.jesp.2021.104198.

US Travel Association. "State of American Vacation 2018." May 8, 2018. ustravel.org/research/state-american-vacation-2018.

Chapter 17: CARE in Leadership

Barton, Michelle A., et al. "Stop Framing Wellness Programs around Self-Care." *Harvard Business Review*, April 4, 2022. hbr.org/2022/04/stop-framing-wellness-programs-around-self-care.

Chadwick, Jonathan. "Two-Thirds of People Laugh at Jokes They Don't Understand to Fit In, with Humour Involving PUNS Puzzling Them the Most, Survey Finds." *Daily Mail Online*, March 5, 2021. dailymail.co.uk/sciencetech/article-9329925/Two-thirds-people-laugh-jokes-dont-understand-fit-survey-finds.html.

Latané, Bibb, and John M. Darley. "Group Inhibition of Bystander Intervention in Emergencies." *Journal of Personality and Social Psychology* vol. 10, no. 3 (1968): 215–21. doi.org/10.1037/h0026570.

About the Author

SARA ROSS is on a mission to help people reignite a sense of aliveness to reshape their work and refuel their lives. She is a keynote speaker and the chief vitality officer of the leadership research firm BrainAmped, where she and her company use brain-science-based strategies to teach people how to amplify their emotional intelligence, resilience, and well-being. Recognized as an expert in the field of leadership, Sara speaks worldwide to companies such as Microsoft, T-Mobile, PepsiCo, FedEx, Bayer, Cisco, BMO, Stanford Health Care, and the US Navy SEALs. Outside of work, Sara is a coffee-loving meditation rookie who lives in Toronto, Canada, with her husband, Mike.

Dear Work, here is how we are changing things...

NOW THAT YOU'RE AT THE END OF THE BOOK, I suspect you have a good idea of what you want to change, either for yourself, your team, or someone you care about who is spinning their wheels in the survival zone.

Here are some ways I can help.

Keynote Speaker for Your Event

Whether a live keynote to a 5,000+ audience, an interactive workshop, or a virtual presentation, I will share how to boost each person's Work Vitality Quotient with the *Dear Work* principles. Visit **saraross.com/keynotes** for topics, delivery options, and media kits.

Bulk Books

Are you looking to purchase books for your whole team, organization, or event? Contact **hello@saraross.com** for bulk discounts and special offers.

Boosting Your Work Vitality Quotient Course

Bold goals. Strong bonds. Big energy. Building on the principles shared in *Dear Work*, I will help you get out of the survival zone and teach you how to fuel your capacity to pursue all three outcomes from your stand-out zone. Full of additional insights and actionable strategies, including a downloadable thirty-day aliveness ignitor framework, this three-part video course with help you reclaim your Work Vitality Quotient. To learn more, go to **dearworkbook.com**.

Monthly Dear Work Letter

Remember, everything counts. Small, simple actions taken consistently over time are how change happens. Sign up for my monthly "Dear Work Letter," where I share exclusive content, strategies, and research to make work better and life fuller. Sign up at **saraross.com/newsletter**.

On-Demand Resources

Interested in additional assessments, research, and resources? Visit **saraross.com**.

One More Thing...

Today with so much information, people are looking for ways to cut through the noise and find what's personally most relevant and helpful. That is what makes reader reviews and recommendations so important.

If you found this book helpful, consider sharing it with others; a few ways to do that include:

- Share or mention the book in blogs, articles, and your social media platforms using **#DearWork** or **#SomethingHasToChange**.

- Submit your rave review to your favorite online book retailer—thank you in advance as they make a huge difference.

- Suggest the book to your friends and family, use it for book clubs, or pick up a copy for those you believe would benefit from the ideas.

- Recommend this book or me, Sara Ross, for events, podcasts, interviews, or anywhere else you believe these ideas can make a difference.